Wedding Vows

Wedding Vows

Beyond Love, Honor, and Cherish

Susan Lee Smith

WARNER BOOKS

A Time Warner Company

Warner Books, Inc., 1271 Avenue of the Americas, New York NY 10020
Visit our Web site at www.twbookmark.com
For information on Time Warner Trade Publishing's online program, visit www.ipublish.com

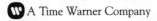 A Time Warner Company

Printed in the United States of America
First Printing: May 2001
10 9 8 7 6 5 4 3 2 1

ISBN: 0-446-67720-5
LCCN: 00-111453

Book design and text composition by Ellen Gleeson
Cover design by Claire Brown
Cover illustration by Leslie Woo

For my mother and father,
who taught me all about
sharing love,
speaking from the heart,
keeping promises,
and living happily ever after.

Contents

Part 1: The Basics

Introduction	3
The Ceremony Location	6
Set the Date First?	6
Geography	7
House of Worship or Not?	9
Indoors or Outdoors?	11
One Location or Two?	15
Get Hitched at City Hall?	17
Happily Ever After, Vegas Style	18
Logistical Considerations	22
Questions to Ask	25
The Officiant	30
Religious vs. Nonreligious Officiants	31
Finding the Right Officiant for You	32
Working with Your Officiant	35
Questions to Ask	37
Wedding Ceremony Structure	40
The Processional	40
The Introduction	40
The Main Body	41

Contents

The Vows 42

The Blessing and Exchange of Ring(s) 42

The Pronouncement 43

The Recessional 43

Who's Giving Whom? 43

Religious Ceremonies 48

Roman Catholic Ceremonies 49

Eastern Orthodox Ceremonies 51

Jewish Ceremonies 52

Protestant Ceremonies 55

Vow Basics 56

Vow Forms 56

Interrogative 56

Directed 56

Monologue 56

Traditional Marriage Vows 59

Religious Vows 59

Buddhist 60

Eastern Orthodox 60

Episcopal 61

Hindu 61

Interfaith (Ecumenical,
Monotheistic) 62

Jewish 62

Contents

Lutheran	63
Muslim	64
Methodist	64
Presbyterian	64
Protestant	65
Roman Catholic	65
Quaker	65
Unitarian/Universalist	66
United Church of Christ	66
Other Religious Vows	67
Nonreligious Vows	67
Interfaith (nonreligious)	68
Civil Ceremony	68
Other Nonreligious Vows	68
Ring Vows	70
Episcopal	70
Jewish	71
Presbyterian	71
Protestant	71
Roman Catholic	72
Quaker	72
Unitarian/Universalist	72
Interfaith Ceremonies	73
Reconciling Religious Issues	77

Contents

Part 2: Personalizing Your Wedding Ceremony

The Personalization Worksheets   85
    Bride's Worksheet   87
    Groom's Worksheet   93

Developing a Theme for Your Ceremony   100
    Theme Worksheet   103

Incorporating Traditions   106
    Bride's Worksheet   107
    Groom's Worksheet   110

Readings   112
    Getting Started   112
    What Kinds of Readings?   113
    Practical Matters   114
    Popular Readings and Writers   116
    Incorporating a Reading into Your Vows   117
    Readings Worksheet   117

Music   120
    Getting Started   120
    What Kind of Music?   121
    Practical Matters   125

Contents

Popular Musical Selections
and Composers   126
Incorporating Song Lyrics into
Your Vows   127
Music Worksheet   127

Writing Your Vows   129
Getting Started   130
Vow Ideas   132
Bride's Worksheet   132
Groom's Worksheet   136
Vow Sources   140
Finding the Right Words   141
The Stuff of Vows   145
Marriage Vows Worksheet—
Traditional Format   146
Ring Vows Worksheet   148
Putting Pen to Paper   149
Writing That Works   151

Part 3: Practical Suggestions

Preparing for the Moment   157

No Plan at All?   162

Contents

A Lasting Reminder   164

Second Weddings and Vow Renewals   167
    "Encore" Weddings   167
    A New Start   169
    Involving Children   170
    Reaffirming or Renewing Your Vows   174

Part 1
The
Basics

Introduction

You (or someone you love) are getting married.

Over two million weddings are held each year in the United States. Remarkably, no two will be exactly alike. Yet whatever the differences—the formality of attire, the kind of flowers, the size of the guest list, the flavor of frosting on the cake—each and every one of those weddings is *guaranteed* to include one element: a ceremony that unites the couple as husband and wife.

In most cases, once an engagement is announced, the planning goes into high gear. The bride searches for the perfect gown. Decisions about invitations, flowers, tuxedos, caterers, and countless other elements must be made. China patterns are weighed against one another, and planning begins for the perfect romantic honeymoon.

In the frenzy of planning wedding events, the ceremony itself—the ritual that joins the bride and groom together—can be overlooked. Yet no part of the day is likely to be more personally meaningful to the couple or more moving to their guests. Ultimately, the ceremony, that exchange of vows, is the very heart and soul of the wedding celebration.

And in an era when interfaith and intercultural marriages are more common than ever before in human history, the ceremony can be a source of anxiety, concern, and even conflict. Making decisions about the ceremony forces a couple to take a position with regard to such important issues as religion, family, history, heritage, duty, honor, and the very essence of their commitment to one another. A couple's decision to have or not have a religious ceremony, to include or not include vows of obedience and fidelity, even the decision about who, if anyone, "gives away" the bride—all these and dozens more can become points of conflict and controversy between the couple and within their families.

For many couples, the right choice is a ceremony that features the exchange of personal vows—either as the sole vows of the ceremony or in addition to more traditional vows. Deciding to write your own vows is relatively easy; but for most couples, actually writing them is tough. Even the most expressive person can end up with a classic case of "writer's block" when faced with finding the right words to express his or her love for a future spouse. Knowing that you will proclaim these vows in front of your closest family and friends usually makes it even more daunting.

It is my hope that this book will help you learn about the possibilities, evaluate the options, make meaningful choices, negotiate past conflicts, quell your own fears, and get what you want—a wonderful wedding ceremony, one that's exactly right for you. I hope it will inspire you to see beyond the "show" of the wedding celebration and focus carefully for a few moments, on what it means to articulate your commitment to one another. I hope the information and advice contained herein will help you get past any anxiety you might have about putting pen to paper and expressing the depth of your feelings for and commitment to your intended. And I hope that the vows you exchange on your wedding day will help guide you each and every day thereafter toward building a great marriage—one filled with comfort, joy, laughter, and, most of all, love.

The Ceremony Location

*W*edding planning experts are largely in agreement that the first thing a couple must decide when planning a wedding is where the ceremony (and reception) will take place. When making this first key decision, it is important to already have an eye toward how your selection of a location may restrict the nature of your ceremony, the substance of your vows, and the duration of your ceremony . . . and vice versa. In particular, your selection of a house of worship or other religious location can mean that many elements of your wedding ceremony will be determined by the practices and policies of that institution.

Set the Date First?

Many couples "set the date," then begin the search. While this approach can work, it may mean that the couple will have to forgo their first choice of location in order to be married on their preferred date. If you simply *must* be married on the third weekend in June, you may find that date already "booked up" at your church, synagogue, or favorite hotel. If a specific ceremony (or reception) location is important to you, consider holding off setting the exact date until you know the availability of that location. Your flexibility about date, as well as time of day, will increase your likelihood of getting a location you really love.

Geography

As you begin to consider locations, deciding where geographically to get married—in what city, town, or wide place in the road—is no longer a foregone conclusion. Several decades ago the average bride and groom were in their early twenties, perhaps just graduated from high school or college (or about to), and a couple most often wed in the bride's hometown. That couple was probably not yet living as independently from their parents as today's average bride and groom are, and the bride's parents were likely carrying the primary financial burden for the wedding. Today's average bride and groom are in their later twenties, with established careers and their own households, and are probably footing the bill themselves for a considerable portion of the wedding. Getting married in the bride's hometown isn't necessarily the logical choice anymore—especially if she hasn't lived there in a decade.

Among the things to consider as you decide in what city you will marry:

※ *Will you logistically be able to plan a wedding in that city?*

If you are planning a wedding long-distance, be prepared for a bigger long-distance phone bill; you will also probably need to travel to that city several times before the big event to finalize important details in person.

❀ *How convenient or inconvenient is that city to the*
people you most want to participate in the wedding?
If the grandparents you adore live in a small town in Georgia two hundred miles from the nearest airport, and you are considering holding your wedding at Yosemite National Forest in California, Grandma and Grandpa will have to endure travel days over twelve hours long each way to attend the event.

❀ *How big a wedding do you want to have (how many*
guests), and how many will need to travel a long dis-
tance to attend?
If you've always dreamed of an enormous event attended by everyone you ever knew growing up, you're best off having the wedding where the largest number of them live. You can probably count on close friends and family traveling great distances to witness your marriage, but more casual acquaintances may not be inclined to plan a flight to join the celebration. If your guest list is all out of state, you're probably looking at a smaller event.

❀ *Are the elements you want available in that city?*

If your wedding day dreams include exchanging vows in a Gothic cathedral, you may not find what you're looking for in beautiful Jackson Hole, Wyoming. If marrying on a majestic mountaintop, overlooking miles of meadows, is your dream, you're going to have to leave New York City.

House of Worship or Not?

Another important consideration—one that will strongly influence your selection of a ceremony location, the vows you exchange, and many other elements of your ceremony—is whether or not you plan to have a religious ceremony. Religion is one of those topics that some people are uncomfortable discussing outside the context of their own spiritual (or nonspiritual) life. However, if you're planning a wedding, it's an unavoidable topic.

The decision about whether or not to have a religious ceremony, whether in a house of worship or a strictly secular location, should be made by the bride and groom alone. Parents may not be pleased; friends may question the decision; but if a couple is mature enough to wed, their choices with regard to religious observance or nonobservance should be respected.

If the bride and groom themselves are at odds about the matter, it must be addressed immediately. A couple's ability to reach an understanding about religious matters is essential not only to planning a meaningful ceremony, but also to countless circumstances that are likely to follow within the marriage itself—from celebrating holidays to child rearing. If there's a problem, work it out now.

The decision about whether or not to have a religious ceremony should stem not from the desire to be married in a particular location, but rather, of course, from a desire to be married within that religious tradition. Some religions require that a marriage take place within a sanctioned house of worship in order to be recognized by the religious body. Others are more flexible on this matter, and the ceremony can take place just about anywhere. Generally speaking, nonreligious locations—hotels, parks, gardens, historic sites, and the like—are available for religious or nonreligious ceremonies. Most houses of worship, on the other hand, have restrictions about who may be married there and what kinds of ceremonies can be performed. While some houses of worship will accommodate nonreligious ceremonies involving nonmembers, those having nonreligious ceremonies will probably be limited to nonreligious locations.

Because the policies vary widely among different religions, denominations, and sects and even among different congregations within a single denomination, the only way to find out if you may be married in a particular house of worship, and the specific conventions or restrictions associated with marrying there, is to ask. If your request to be married in a particular house of worship is declined, don't hesitate to ask why. It may be that by attending classes or converting to that faith, you may be married there. Certainly it is not advisable to "take on" a faith simply to secure a ceremony location; however, if your commitment is true, this may be the perfect opportunity to strengthen your spiritual life. If instead the bottom line is that you and the house of worship just aren't going to see eye to eye, move on. There are many lovely places to hold your ceremony; you can find one that shares your sensibilities.

In the United States, religious institutions are increasingly asking those who wish to be married within the religious community to participate in some kind of prewedding marriage preparation course, conducted either by the resident officiant or through a related organization or group. In some cases participation is optional; in other cases it is mandatory. The sooner you understand the expectations of the house of worship where you plan to marry, the better. Arrange to meet with the officiant or other official at your earliest convenience to discuss your plans and clarify expectations. At this first meeting you should also plan to discuss what restrictions, if any, the institution has with regard to the vows you will recite, musical selections, readings, and all other elements of your ceremony.

Indoors or Outdoors?

The most obvious consideration when deciding whether or not to have an indoor or outdoor ceremony is weather. Weather predicting has become very sophisticated, and you can find numerous so-called authorities that will predict the weather in your wedding city on your projected wedding date . . . but don't count on it. We all know that these predictions are far from 100 percent accurate. You should always have a backup plan if you are planning an outdoor event.

If you are planning a wedding in colder climes during winter, be practical. Even if the weather is clear, the temperature is likely to be too chilly outdoors for most of your guests. Different regions of the country are prone to rainy weather during the spring, so plan accordingly. Other areas experience high humidity during the summer and early fall; your guests may melt if asked to sit through an outdoor ceremony.

Don't just consider the weather in terms of the magic moment itself; snow, ice, and rain can also create havoc on the roadways and impede your guests, vendors, and service providers or even your own ability to make it to the event on time . . . or at all.

If you are considering an outdoor wedding, you should realize that there are other variables than the weather that may be beyond your control. The location may be subject to disruptive or distracting noises or sounds. A wedding in a civic garden may seem the perfect idea—but what if you arrive at the location on the big day only to discover a road crew tearing up the neighboring city street with jackhammers? Will low-flying jets drown out your vows? If you plan to marry outside, visit the location at the chosen time of day, on the same day of the week, to gauge the ambient decibels. Bring a picnic basket and stay awhile. Check with local authorities to make sure there isn't a major demolition project or public parade scheduled at or near the site on your special day.

If your outdoor location is a public one—such as a city park—be aware that your event may be interrupted by the public. When you book the location, make sure there is a clear understanding of the specific boundaries of the area you are to use, how the boundaries will be enforced, and what other events or public access will be allowed to take place adjacent to that location on the day of your wedding. Even if a passerby is just curious, he or she might unwittingly interrupt or intrude upon the event. If that is a concern, you must take steps in advance to secure the perimeter of the location, which may mean hiring a private security service.

An outdoor location might also present obstacles to participants or guests with health concerns—particularly those with allergies or physical limitations that might make it difficult for them to reach the location. If you're planning to marry amid an alpine meadow in the pristine Idaho wilderness, make sure in advance that your officiant won't have a sneezing attack and that your dearest great-aunt who uses a walker will have a way to the spot without trouble.

Finally, there are the two essentials for a wedding that might not be in ready supply if you plan to wed out of doors: electricity and rest rooms. Don't laugh. It's difficult to have a wedding without the first, and *please* don't try to have one without the second.

With regard to the ceremony, electricity can be essential for lighting, musical equipment, and sound equipment. Planning on having a candlelit ceremony, engaging an a cappella choir, and just speaking loudly? Okay, you can probably forgo electricity, but make sure you have authorization to have open flames, and have an emergency fire plan in case something goes wrong. Electricity may also be essential for your photographer and videographer, so if you really plan to have your ceremony sans electricity, make sure all your vendors and service providers are aware of this limitation. Keep in mind that if you will need to rent and use a generator to power your event, you may have a noise problem; most generators are quite loud.

As for rest rooms . . . well, there's just no doing without them, especially if your location is for both the ceremony and the reception. If your outdoor location has rest room facilities, make sure they are in good working order and that their plumbing is sufficient for an event of your size and duration. Expect that each guest will need to use the facilities about once every three hours. If you will need to rent portable rest rooms in order to stage that wedding on that long stretch of deserted beachfront, keep in mind that each unit typically reaches capacity after 115 uses. If only your ceremony will take place in that location, you can probably get away with just two rest rooms—one for women and one for men. (Two might seem excessive, but it also provides you with a solution should one malfunction.) If your location will be used for the ceremony and the reception, and your combined events will last four to five hours, you should plan on a minimum of two rest rooms per 150 guests. For each hour past five hours that your event will last, count on needing one additional rest room.

One Location or Two?

Before you begin to visit potential ceremony locations, you should take some time to consider whether you prefer to have your ceremony in one location and the reception in another or to have both events in a single location. Each approach has its own advantages and possible drawbacks.

One Location (for Both Ceremony and Reception)
- ❋ Participants will not have to travel or risk becoming lost between locations
- ❋ Celebration feels more like one big event than two separate events
- ❋ Parking/valet arrangements need to be made for only one site
- ❋ Ceremony decorations (such as flowers) can be easily repurposed for reception
- ❋ If house of worship: location ideal for ceremony site may not include restaurant, catering, or ballroom-type facilities
- ❋ If house of worship: location may restrict the serving of alcohol, other beverages, or menu selections
- ❋ May be more difficult to have different guest lists for ceremony and reception

❀ May save on invitation costs by eliminating need for reception insert cards
❀ Guests may be less inclined to skip ceremony and attend only reception
❀ Guests may be inclined to linger around the ceremony area (observing photo taking, taking photos themselves, and so on) rather than proceed on to reception area
❀ If other weddings are being held on-site after your ceremony, guests attending other weddings may mistake your reception event for the one they are attending

Two Locations (One for Ceremony, Another for Reception)
❀ Easier to create a ceremony that is distinct from the reception (for example, a serious, elegant ceremony contrasted with a casual, over-the-top reception)
❀ Allows for ceremony in a house of worship, followed by a reception in a secular location, which may be better suited for a partylike celebration
❀ Participants will have to travel between locations
❀ Parking/valet arrangements will possibly need to be made for two sites
❀ Easier to have different guest lists for ceremony and reception
❀ Need for reception insert cards in wedding invitations will probably mean higher overall invitations costs

❋ Guests may be more inclined to skip ceremony
and attend only reception

Get Hitched at City Hall?

For many couples, the perfect wedding is a civil ceremony. And if you think a civil ceremony necessarily
means the bride and groom alone making a quick trip to
City Hall, guess again; today's civil ceremony can be
short and sweet or as elaborate as the traditional church
or synagogue ceremony. The key distinguishing factor in
a civil ceremony is who performs the service: a civil
authority (as opposed to a religious one). Depending on
the laws of your state, that might mean a judge, a mayor,
a justice of the peace, superior court or county clerk, or
other official, whether elected or appointed. To find out
who is authorized to perform civil ceremonies in your
area, contact your local marriage license–issuing office.

If you wish to be wed, for example, by your local justice
of the peace, and that meets your county's requirements,
your next step is to contact the justice directly to find out
your options for when and where such a ceremony might
take place. You may be required to bring two additional
adults to witness your ceremony, or the civil authority may
be able to provide sufficient witnesses for you. Be sure to
inquire what flexibility you might have as to the nature of
the ceremony—if you may create your own vows and so
forth—and find out the officiant's fee. Most states do not
allow judges to charge a fee for performing ceremonies

during regular business hours, but after hours, on week-ends, and on court holidays, they may charge a fee. While civil ceremonies often take place in civic offices, many couples today opt to have a civil authority perform their ceremony at a more conventional (albeit secular) ceremony location; all you need to do is locate a civil authority who is willing to perform your ceremony "on location."

Happily Ever After, Vegas Style

For many couples, especially those with budget concerns or who want to "get hitched quick," Las Vegas is *the* way to wed. Whether the celebration will include just the bride and groom or be extended to include family members or friends, Vegas offers many options. The revitalization and diversification of Las Vegas as a travel destination, and the addition of extravagant (even out-landish) new hotels, mean that a Vegas wedding no longer necessarily means a quickie ceremony at a neon-lit chapel. If a Vegas wedding is what you have in mind, consider the following:

❋Most of the big hotels offer wedding packages that include accommodations, use of an on-site chapel (bigger hotels may have more than one), and a range of amenities, usually including a wedding coordinator who will handle all the details. If you have guests who need accommodations, you may be able to negotiate a reduced group rate for your rooms.

❋ Wedding chapels similarly offer packages that include flowers, wedding gown and tuxedo rental, and even salon-style hair and makeup services. When you make your arrangements, make sure you have an explicit understanding of what is or isn't included and what any extras will cost.

❋ Historically, the appeal of a Vegas wedding was that it could be fast, and even now there is no waiting period for a marriage license in Nevada (which currently will set you back $35 from the Clark County Clerk's Office). No medical exam is required. Men and women must be at least eighteen years of age, although a license will be granted to a bride or groom sixteen or over with parental consent.

❋ With regard to your ceremony: Most chapels will only permit the ceremony to be performed by their "in house" officiant, so you should keep in mind that your Vegas wedding will probably be nonreligious and your ability to personalize the ceremony (by including your own vows, for example) will probably be limited.

For more information:

Marriage Licenses

Clark County Clerk
309 S. Third St., 3rd floor
Las Vegas, NV 89115
702-455-3156

Wedding Chapels

Little Chapel of the Flowers
800-843-2410
www.littlechapel.com

Little White Wedding Chapel
800-545-8111
www.marryme2000.com

Viva Las Vegas Chapel
800-574-4450
www.vivalasvegasweddings.com

Hotels That Include Wedding Chapels

Bellagio
888-464-4436
www.bellagiolasvegas.com

Caesars Palace
800-634-6001
www.caesars.com

Mandalay Bay
877-632-7701
www.mandalaybay.com

MGM Grand
888-646-1203
www.mgmgrand.com/lv

Monte Carlo
800-822-8651
www.monte-carlo.com

Paris, Las Vegas
877-796-2092
www.paris-lv.com

Treasure Island
800-866-4748
www.treasureisland.com

Tropicana
800-325-5839
www.tropicanachapel.com

Venetian
877-883-6423
www.venetian.com

Logistical Considerations

In ancient Greece, January was considered the ideal month in which to be wed. Victorian England popularized the concept of the June wedding—so that even now we continue to speak of "the June bride." In America today, June is no longer the most popular month for weddings; statistics tell us that May is. Still, spring into summer weddings remain the most common—no doubt owing to weather considerations. A whopping 70 percent of all weddings take place between May and September. More weddings during that time of year mean a greater demand for ceremony locations. So time of year is just one of the factors to consider when selecting your wedding date.

Your first consideration in selecting a month or season in which to marry is timing: How soon do you want to wed, and can you plan a wedding in the amount of time available to you? Experts recommend you give yourself a full year to plan. That's a generous allotment, but if you are planning an elaborate event, have career or other obligations that place significant demands on your time, or simply must have a particular date and location, you should indeed give yourself a year to plan. If you have less time, you may want to aim for a smaller, less complicated event.

Another consideration, as mentioned already, is weather. A Christmas wedding may sound perfect, but if you plan to marry in Wisconsin, dare you risk that snow will keep guests from making it to the church on time? If you have your heart set on marrying in your native

Louisiana, an August wedding might be a bad idea, unless humidity doesn't bother you, your family, and your friends. Only you can know just how weather-resistant you and your guests are. Consider the weather when selecting a date.

If you wish to marry in your church, synagogue, or other house of worship, be sure to speak with your officiant as soon as possible. Most religious institutions give preference to members and/or their children. Still, popular locations or institutions with large congregations can become booked up months in advance. And other events to be held in the facilities or on the grounds might conflict with your desired schedule. The sooner you can meet and secure a date, the better.

Also be aware that in some cases religious law may dictate restrictions on when you may be wed and who may participate in or witness the event. For example, Jewish weddings are traditionally not to be held on the Jewish Sabbath, from sundown on Friday to sundown on Saturday, or on other holy days. However, different branches and even different rabbis may interpret the parameters of the Sabbath differently, so you should check with your synagogue or rabbi to learn the specific restrictions. In the Church of Jesus Christ of Latter-day Saints (the Mormons), only church members in good standing may attend a temple ceremony, so many Mormon couples have a second celebration in another location that all guests may attend.

If you are planning to be married somewhere other

than in a religious building, you should still attempt to secure a location as early in the planning process as possible. Civic facilities, including parks, museums, and gardens, may have annual or special events that limit the scheduling of weddings. State or federal holidays may also put restrictions on availability. Hotels will generally not present obstacles based on religious or civic laws, but their calendar will include other weddings, receptions, parties, balls, conventions, seminars, meetings, and the like.

If budget is a serious consideration (and for most couples it is), you might also look to schedule your wedding around major holidays that might impact the availability and costs for the elements that will constitute your big event. For example, flowers, and roses in particular, are in highest demand, and thus are the most expensive, around Valentine's Day and Mother's Day. Avoid these dates if your dreamy ceremony takes place beneath an elaborate rose-covered *chuppah*. Hotel ballrooms, caterers, bands, and disc jockeys are typically busiest around Christmas and New Year's Eve, booked up with holiday parties and New Year's celebrations. These providers, as well as limousine companies, may also be heavily booked in May and June with school proms and graduation parties, so plan accordingly.

Another important logistical consideration is what time of day to hold your event. Your decision is not a trivial one. Among the factors that will likely be influenced by your choice:

Costs. Generally speaking, your wedding costs (especially reception costs) will be less if your wedding is earlier in the day. If you are the average couple, just over 30 percent of your wedding budget will go toward food and beverages for your guests at the reception. People are more likely to imbibe alcohol in the evening than they are in the morning, and dinner fare is more expensive than brunch.

Formality. Traditionally, evening weddings are the most formal; while you can feel free to hold a formal wedding any time of day, and you may certainly hold a casual celebration in the evening, your guests are likely to anticipate a formal ceremony if your wedding is held at six P.M. or later. A higher degree of formality will affect the selection (and relative cost) of invitations, wedding party attire, and nearly every detail of the reception—from the food to the entertainment.

Lighting. There's no law that says you can't have a candlelit ceremony in the morning (unless, of course, your ceremony location or fire codes specifically prohibit it), but the drama of candlelight is likely to be lost in the bright light of day. Similarly, if you have always imagined a seaside wedding, beneath the blue sky, beside the shimmering water, you don't want an evening wedding.

Questions to Ask

When you contact a potential ceremony location, you'll want to be prepared with a complete set of questions that will enable you to better understand whether or not that location is appropriate for you.

In addition to questions that address your specific circumstances and needs, you may want to ask the following:

- ❉ Is the location indoors, outdoors, or a combination of the two? Please describe.
- ❉ What is the maximum seated capacity of the location? Is there seating for that number of people, or will seating have to be brought in?
- ❉ What parking is available? How many vehicles can be parked? Is there a fee? How far will participants have to walk from the parking to the ceremony site? Is that walkway open or covered? Is there handicapped parking and handicapped access from the parking area?
- ❉ What other events will be held at that location the same day? How many? At what times will each begin and conclude?
- ❉ How long is the location available before the start of the event for setting up decorations, equipment, and the like? How long is the location available after the conclusion of the event for breaking down decorations, equipment, and so on?
- ❉ Do you provide an on-site coordinator for the day of the event? May I meet that person in advance of the event?
- ❉ Is the location available prior to the event so we may hold a rehearsal? When (day and time)? For how long?

❀ Which areas are we specifically allowed to use?
Are any areas off limits?

❀ What are the rest room facilities? How many?
Where are they located?

❀ Is there handicapped/wheelchair access to the site?
Are there handicapped rest rooms?

❀ Is there a phone or pay phone on the premises that
we can use, if necessary, the day of the event?

❀ Are there rooms available for the wedding party
members to dress and/or prepare for the event?
How many? Where? Do those facilities include rest
rooms? Electrical outlets? Full-length (or other
size) mirrors?

❀ Is there a place to lock up the wedding party's
belongings (purses and so on) during the ceremony?

❀ Are there any restrictions on who can officiate the
ceremony?

❀ Are there any restrictions on what kind of ceremony
can be performed?

❀ Is there lighting? What kind? What areas does it
illuminate? Is the illumination sufficient for an
evening wedding? Are candles permitted?

❀ Is there a sound system? If not, are the acoustics
good enough that guests will be able to hear the
service without a sound system? May a sound system be brought in?

❀ Is electricity available for additional lighting,
sound equipment, and so on? Where and how
much? Are cables provided?

❀ Are there any restrictions with regard to decorating the location?

❀ Are there any restrictions with regard to taking photographs and video?

❀ Are there any restrictions with regard to attire (for the wedding party and/or for guests)?

❀ Are there any music resources on-site—for example, a piano? Are there any restrictions about who may use such resources?

❀ How long have you been in business? Under this management?

❀ What is the fee for the location? Paid in what manner/on what schedule?

❀ What is your cancellation policy?

If the location is a house of worship or other religious site, you may also want or need to ask the following:

❀ Must the bride and/or the groom be a member of this congregation?

❀ Must the bride and/or the groom practice this faith?

❀ Are there any special requirements of the bride and groom in order to be married in this location (such as baptism, conversion, premarriage counseling/classes)?

❀ What are the options as to type of ceremony? Approximately how long will the ceremony run?

❀ Are there any restrictions as to who performs the

ceremony? Must a resident officiant perform the ceremony, or may an outside officiant preside?

※ If applicable: May more than one officiant perform the ceremony together? May a nonreligious officiant perform the ceremony, either alone or with another officiant?

※ If applicable: Are there any restrictions with regard to interfaith ceremonies?

※ Are there any rites or practices that are not permitted?

※ Are there any restrictions with regard to the use of religious scriptures or specific translations?

※ Are there any restrictions as to who may attend the event?

The Officiant

If the bride and groom are the stars of the wedding ceremony, then the officiant surely plays the "best supporting" role. However, your choice of an officiant is important on more than just a superficial, theatrical level. Depending on your beliefs and practices, your officiant may very well serve a sacred role in conducting your marriage ceremony; he or she may be your spiritual guide during the months leading up to your wedding and may continue to play a significant role in your lives beyond the big event. Even if you are having a secular ceremony, your officiant has great power to set the tenor of the ceremony itself—from serious and thoughtful to jubilant and even humorous. He or she will occupy a central place in the event, presiding over the event and guiding you through the ceremony that unites you as husband and wife. As you assemble the elements of your wedding day, keep in mind that the selection of the right officiant, and your ability to work with your officiant to create the ceremony that's right for you, is essential.

Religious vs. Nonreligious Officiants

If you have an active spiritual life, and especially if you and your betrothed share your religious observance, you may already know exactly whom you want to have perform your wedding ceremony: the rabbi, priest, minister, or other religious figure who leads your regular religious practice. If you don't wish to have a religious ceremony, you will probably not have too much difficulty finding a civil authority to perform your secular wedding. Arguably the most challenging positions to be in are those of the nonactive persons of faith who wish to have a religious ceremony or the couple seeking an interfaith ceremony. But whatever your circumstances, if you start early and approach the matter thoughtfully, you'll be able to find just the right officiant for your wedding celebration.

Generally speaking, the lines are neatly drawn: An officiant affiliated with a particular religious institution will perform ceremonies within the parameters defined by that institution, for couples who practice that faith; civil authorities will perform secular ceremonies for couples regardless of their religious affiliation (or nonaffiliation), although individual secular officiants may be willing to include elements or references from religious practice (such as invoking God, leading prayers, and the like). Some religious officiants are open to performing ceremonies for nonobservant couples and for couples seeking interfaith ceremonies, which the officiant performs either alone or in conjunction with an officiant from the other religion. Many interfaith couples choose to have a nonreligious ceremony or one with references to only those elements of their respective faiths that are shared, performed by a civil authority. The only way to find out for sure what an officiant—religious or secular—can or will do is to ask.

If a religious officiant will not perform your ceremony, or will not perform the kind of ceremony you want, you should accept his or her decision graciously and move on. There's no reason to "take it personally." Keep in mind that he or she has dedicated his or her life to serving God and the religious institution. As important as your wedding is to you, it probably will not cause an officiant to abandon his or her deeply held beliefs and religious obligations. Keep in mind too that the obstacle may be the guidelines set down by the larger religious institution. You may want to ask the declining officiant the reason for his or her decision and if he or she has any advice or suggestions as to how you can successfully bring together the wedding ceremony you have in mind.

Finding the Right Officiant for You

Finding the right officiant starts with making some basic decision about what kind of ceremony you want to have. Even if you wish to have a lighthearted celebration, your ceremony is important and deserves as much (if not more) careful thought than any other element of your wedding day.

If you want to have a religious ceremony, and

. . . your desire to be married at a particular religious location supersedes other considerations, you should inquire with that location before securing an officiant. There may be a policy that the presiding officiant of that house of worship is the only person who can perform wedding ceremonies there.

. . . your desire to be married by a particular officiant supersedes other considerations, meet with that officiant right away to find out where he or she is allowed to perform weddings; with any luck, it'll be a location you love.

. . . you would like to have a ceremony within your current house of worship, meet with the presiding officiant to discuss available dates and what options (or restrictions) exist for your ceremony.

. . . you don't currently have a house of worship, you may want to start your search for an officiant by looking for houses of worship (within your religion or denomination of choice) in a local phone directory. Attend regular worship services, noting (discreetly—after all, you're there to worship) whether or not the location and officiant might be right for you. Once you have found the right location and/or officiant, you should meet with the officiant as soon as possible to discuss your interest in becoming more involved in the institution and being married there. If you're interested in the house of worship only for the purposes of your wedding, that will probably quickly become apparent to the officiant and may become a source of conflict. Be honest about your intentions, and don't feign interest in a house of worship just to secure a ceremony location or officiant.

If you want to have an interfaith religious ceremony, and

. . . you and your betrothed are each active in your respective houses of worship, you should meet with your officiants as soon as possible to explain your intention to marry and discuss to what degree each officiant and institution is willing to be involved in your wedding celebration (presuming that you will wish to marry in one location or the other and that you would like your ceremony performed by your two officiants).

. . . only one of you is currently active in your house of worship, meet with that officiant as soon as possible to discuss the availability of the house of worship for an interfaith ceremony and if the officiant can perform an interfaith ceremony; if he or she can perform interfaith ceremonies, he or she may be able to recommend an officiant from the other faith to join him or her in performing the ceremony.

. . . neither of you is currently active in a house of worship, you each should start your search for a house of worship or officiant with an eye toward finding not only the one you like, but one who will permit an interfaith ceremony.

. . . you are unable, after repeated efforts, to find an institution or officiants willing to perform an interfaith ceremony, you may want to consider having a civil (non-religious) ceremony instead.

If you want to have a nonreligious ceremony, you should contact your local marriage license office to find out who may legally perform your wedding ceremony. Your local phone directory may have listings of officiants who perform civil ceremonies, or you may find that the coordinator at your ceremony location can recommend someone to perform your civil ceremony.

Working with Your Officiant

Your officiant wants to help you create a meaningful ceremony. Whether you already have a relationship with your officiant or are meeting him or her for the first time to discuss your wedding plans, there's only one way to make sure he or she understands your preferences: You need to be able to articulate your thoughts and feelings about your wedding ceremony. Most officiants want to get to know the bride and groom and may require the couple to meet with him or her several times in the months leading up to the wedding. These meetings really are for the couple's benefit: The better your officiant knows you—individually and as a couple—the more personal he or she can make your ceremony. In addition to one-on-one meetings with your officiant, you may be required to attend premarital counseling classes if you plan to marry within a particular religious tradition. If these classes are conducted by the officiant performing your ceremony, it will be another chance for him or her to become better acquainted with the two of you.

Wedding Vows

Some couples who are planning a religious ceremony—particularly those who are not active in observing their faith—are nervous about interacting with their officiant and fear that problems will arise because they are "not devout enough." Others go so far as to put on a show of faith in an effort to appease the officiant. Concerns about "measuring up" to the officiant's standards are generally unfounded, and a couple is strongly advised against playing up to the officiant. He or she is really interested only in a genuine commitment to faith and will probably see through any ruse. Still, exercise good judgment, don't flaunt your casual association to the institution, and show at least polite respect for its traditions.

In your first meeting with your officiant (or officiants), you will want to find out what restrictions, if any, there are on the substance of your ceremony, including the vows you may exchange and readings or music that may be performed. You will want to ask for a copy of the recommended or approved ceremony, with a clear indication of what elements, if any, may be eliminated or replaced and if the order of elements may be changed. Listen carefully to your officiant's explanations. If there are elements of the ceremony that you are not comfortable with, state your concerns. Explain why "doing it that way" will make the ceremony less personally relevant and meaningful for you; this is usually a much stronger argument than just saying that you don't like it or don't want it. For example, some couples prefer that biblical readings come from a modern translation that contains gender-neutral language. This stems from their desire to express the egalitarian nature of their relationship. If you frame your concerns to your officiant in the context of how doing it the traditional way will make the ceremony less meaningful to you, you may find your officiant willing to work with you to find an alternative. Enter the discussions with an open mind, listen carefully to your officiant's position, and whenever possible seek a compromise.

Questions to Ask

You'll likely have a long list of questions to ask your officiant—and he or she will have lots of questions for you. Your goal is to understand the substance of the ceremony, its conventions or restrictions, and what flexibility there might be to "personalize" the ceremony. Your officiant's goal is to get to know you better as a couple, perhaps to ensure that you are prepared to take this step, and to help you create a truly meaningful ceremony. Here are some questions you may want to ask a potential officiant and/or officiant who will perform your ceremony (whether religious or secular), plus several you may want to ask a religious officiant.

Any Officiant
* Are you available to perform a ceremony (date, time, location if already determined)?
* Where are you able to perform a ceremony (if location not already determined)?

❋ Are you available to perform a rehearsal in advance of the ceremony?

❋ What are the options as to type of ceremony? What elements are normally included? How much flexibility do we have in creating the ceremony? Can any of the elements of the ceremony be eliminated or replaced? Can the order of the ceremony elements be changed?

❋ Are there any special requirements of the bride and groom in order to be married by you (such as premarital counseling)?

❋ If applicable: Are you willing to co-officiate a ceremony? Under what circumstances and/or with what restrictions?

❋ What is your fee?

Religious Officiants

❋ Must the bride and/or the groom practice your faith?

❋ Must the bride and/or the groom be a member of the congregation of your house of worship?

❋ Are there any commitments that the couple must make in order to be married by you (for example, to raise any children they have within a particular faith)?

❋ If applicable: Are you willing to perform an interfaith ceremony? Are you willing to co-officiate the ceremony with an officiant of another faith?

❋ Are any rites or practices required in order for you

to perform the ceremony? Any that are not permitted if you perform the ceremony?

❀ Are there any restrictions with regard to the use of
religious scriptures or specific translations?

❀ Are there any restrictions as to who may participate in the ceremony (for example, as a reader)?
As to who may attend the event?

Wedding Ceremony Structure

*I*n Western or Eurocentric weddings—which predominate in the United States—the ceremony typically follows a common structure, although the elements may change or the order may shift depending on religion or denomination, ethnic influences, geographical region, the formality of the service, or the simple preference of the couple. Although this ceremony has its roots in the Judeo-Christian religious tradition, it has become the shared structure of Western religious and secular ceremonies alike.

The basic structure of most Western wedding ceremonies, with the elements in their most familiar order, is as follows:

❋ **The processional.** The members of the wedding party, and the officiant(s), enter the ceremony location, culminating with the entrance of the bride.

❋ **The introduction, convocation, opening, or greeting.** The officiant announces the purpose of the gathering, mentions the bride and groom by name, welcomes the guests to the celebration, and encourages them to serve as witnesses to the union, perhaps participating in responsive readings and in unison or silent prayers. At a religious ceremony, this might also include an **invocation,** wherein the officiant calls upon God to be present and bless the union that will be created in this celebration.

✾ **The main body.** The officiant will share his or her thoughts and perhaps the institution's teachings on the meaning of marriage, which may take the form of a short **sermon** or **homily.** He or she will likely share personal remarks about the bride and groom, their immediate families, and the goodness that is created in the couple choosing to join together in marriage. This portion of the ceremony might also include religious or other readings by the officiant or by others whom the bride and groom have asked to speak. This portion of the service usually includes the **interrogation** and the **presentation.** The **interrogation** is when the officiant asks the couple if they have come to marry of their own free will and usually includes some form of "expression of intent," in which the bride and groom verbally acknowledge their desire to be joined in marriage. The interrogation may also include a question to the congregation—the question that is usually followed by a silence so great, you can hear a corsage pin drop: "If anyone has just cause why these two may not wed, speak now or forever hold your peace." The interrogation is usually then followed by (although the order is sometimes switched) the **presentation**, in which the bride, or the bride and groom, are presented for marriage by their parents, their family members, or, as is sometimes the case in second weddings, their children from previous relationships (see sidebar "Who's Giving Whom?")

❋ **The vows.** The officiant ruminates on the significance of the vows that the couple is going to exchange; then the bride and groom individually express and affirm their commitment to one another, usually either by repeating phrases at the direction of the officiant or by responding to questions posed by the officiant; the responses usually take the form of "I do" or "I will." Increasingly, couples are augmenting these vows with spoken statements from the bride and groom declaring their love.

❋ **The blessing and exchange of ring(s).** The bride and groom take turns repeating phrases at the officiant's direction, each declaring their commitment to one another and expressing the symbolic meaning of the ring while placing it on the hand of his or her betrothed. In some cases only the bride receives a ring, but for several generations now it has been popular to have a double ring ceremony, in which the groom also receives a ring.

❋ **The pronouncement.** The officiant announces that the couple is officially wed. This may also include a final prayer, benediction, or religious rite (such as the Jewish custom of the breaking of the glass). The officiant may indicate that the groom may "kiss the bride," and/or the officiant may introduce the newly married couple to the congregation.

❋ **The recessional.** Led by the bride and groom, the wedding party members exit the location.

Who's Giving Whom?

Traditionally, it's one of the "big moments" of any wedding—when the bride is walked down the aisle and "given away" in marriage (known more formally as "the presentation"). But this tradition, like many others, has come under intense scrutiny in the last several decades. The giving away of the bride—whether we speak strictly of the act of escorting the bride down the aisle or the verbal response to the question "Who gives this woman to be married to this man?"—makes some modern brides (and other participants as well) uncomfortable.

Admittedly, this tradition may seem to smack of the worst of our patriarchal past, in which a young woman was viewed as "property" handed from one man (her father or, in some traditions, both her parents) to another (her new husband). So what is today's independent woman to do about this potentially sticky moment in the ceremony?

The matter is further complicated by the fact that a bride today may recognize more than one man as having played a key role in her upbringing; she may have a father and a stepfather who she feels equally "deserve" the honor of escorting her down the aisle. Or she may have no father figure at all and be at a loss for how to handle this moment in the ceremony.

To decide what's right for you, consider the following:

❊ **Let ancient history be ancient history.**
Just because a tradition started for questionable reasons doesn't mean you have to let that color your moment. If the bride wishes to be given away in the traditional manner, she should feel free to take the traditional approach; it doesn't make her any less modern, independent, or enlightened.

❊ **Leave traditions you don't like in the dust.**
If the bride doesn't care for any part of the

presentation, it need not be included. The bride can walk down the aisle alone, and (presuming the officiant or institution is in agreement) the line "Who gives this woman . . ." need not be read. Your guests will probably not even notice the omission.

※ **The more the merrier.** You can have more than one person walk you down the aisle. In fact, in the Jewish tradition the bride is escorted by both her parents. A bride with more than one father or father figure whom she wishes to recognize can have both of them walk her down the aisle (although once there is more than one on each arm, things can get tricky). Be sure to consider the width and length of the aisle you will be walking down when making the decision to have multiple simultaneous escorts, and be sure to rehearse this moment in the actual location.

※ **Consider the bride relay.** If two (or more) simultaneous escorts won't work, the bride might consider having different escorts walk her down different segments of the aisle. One California bride who was close to her biological father in the earliest years of her life but even closer to the stepfather who adopted her as a teenager had her biological father walk her down the first half of the aisle (representing the earlier years of her life) and her adoptive father walk her the rest of the way down the aisle.

❋ **Who says it has to be Dad?** Keep in mind that the person who escorts the bride down the aisle and/or makes the verbal presentation need not be her father or, for that matter, a male member of her family. Not only can Mom fit the bill, but so can a beloved grandparent, sibling, aunt or uncle, or close friend, especially one who has served as a mentor to the bride. As previously mentioned, the bride can just walk herself down the aisle, no escort required. Brides who are already mothers often have their children walk them down the aisle.

❋ **Play on the words.** If you're concerned about what your escort will say in response to the officiant's inquiry "Who gives this woman to be married (un)to this man?" you might want to consider the following alternatives.

To make Mom feel more included: "Her mother and I do."

To recognize the bride's self-determination: "She gives herself, with our [or 'my' or 'her parents' or 'her family's'] blessing."

Instead of "Who gives this woman . . ." you may wish to substitute "Who brings this woman . . ." or "Who presents this woman . . . "

One final note: Giving away the bride is something that many fathers (and mothers) look forward to from the moment a daughter is born. For most, the presentation of the bride is not a politically tainted legacy, but a powerful moment in the relationship between a parent (or parents) and a beloved daughter. No bride should participate in a ritual she finds offensive; however, she should think carefully before denying her parent or parents the opportunity to participate in a ritual that celebrates this important life passage.

Religious Ceremonies

*W*ithin our borders virtually every world religion is observed. To summarize and represent the wedding traditions of every religion practiced on U.S. soil would require volumes, so the overview provided here merely addresses the religions most widely practiced. Your best resource for the detailed information on the specific practices of any house of worship is that institution's own staff. Keep in mind that there can be differences in belief and practice even within a single denomination or sect. If you're looking to create a highly personalized ceremony within the framework of a religious institution, you may be met with some challenges; although policies vary widely, most religious traditions include a fairly structured wedding ceremony. The institution will likely have a list of ceremony elements that must be included, but you may have some latitude to add other, more personal elements, as long as they don't conflict with the religion's beliefs and practices.

Roman Catholic Ceremonies

In the Roman Catholic Church, marriage is one of the seven holy sacraments, meaning that it is among the most important ceremonies performed by the church; thus the wedding ceremony is conducted within defined parameters, including elements of the regular mass service. Although exceptions might sometimes be made, one such restriction is that the service, a nuptial mass, must take place within a consecrated Catholic church. The priest who will perform your ceremony will discuss the matter with you in more detail, including what options might be available to you in terms of a Catholic wedding service.

The element of the nuptial mass that weds the couple is the rite of marriage. In the typical Catholic wedding celebration, the marriage rite occurs within a sequence of other rites, liturgies, and sacraments. Specifically, the common order of rites in the nuptial mass are as follows:

* **The gathering and entrance rite,** in which the celebrant or priest leads the processional, greets the guests, and invokes God's blessing upon the couple, their families, and all gathered for the event.
* **The penitential rite,** in which the celebrant or priest leads a communal prayer for mercy and for-giveness, usually followed by the singing of the Gloria; in some cases this rite may be deleted from the nuptial mass proceedings.
* **The liturgy of the Word,** which is a series of four

readings from the Bible: the first from the Hebrew Bible or Old Testament; the second a psalm (which can be spoken or sung); the third from the non-Gospel books of the New Testament. Then, following the singing of the Alleluia prayer or Gospel Acclamation, there is a reading from one of the four Gospels (the first four books of the New Testament—Matthew, Mark, Luke, and John). The congregation traditionally stands for the reading of the Gospel. The readings are selected by the couple in consort with the priest and traditionally address topics relevant to the circumstances—reflections on love, marriage, and family. The priest will also deliver a short homily on these subjects.

❀ **The marriage rite,** which includes an expression of intent by the bride and groom, the exchange of vows and rings, and a series of prayers. Those prayed for may include the couple, their families (those present, those not present, and those who may have passed away), those congregated to witness the event, and the larger communities beyond. If the bride and groom are both Catholics, the marriage rite spiritually culminates with the Eucharist, or Communion sacrament. The Communion host is blessed, and the congregation recites the Lord's Prayer. The congregation exchanges greetings, handshakes, or hugs as a sign of peace, the host is distributed, and Communion is received. For interfaith weddings, there is a version of the rite of marriage that is conducted out-side of the mass service and does not include Communion.

※ **The concluding rite,** in which blessings are said for the couple and the community, and the priest dismisses those gathered. The recessional follows, and once the wedding party and priest have left, the guests are free to exit.

Eastern Orthodox Ceremonies

As in the Catholic Church, the wedding ceremony is a sacrament in the Eastern Orthodox tradition, although the Eastern Orthodox ceremony is not a mass service. The ceremony includes a number of rituals performed in "threes"—repeated three times to symbolically represent the Holy Trinity of Father, Son, and Holy Spirit. Before the bride and groom enter the church, the priest con-ducts the **betrothal**, in which the rings are blessed, placed on the bride's and groom's hands, then switched three times. Within the church, the bride and groom each carry a lit candle, and the priest performs the marriage sacrament, which does not include spoken vows by the couple. Rather, the key element of the ceremony is the **crowning**, during which *stafana*, or crowns, usually made of metal, are placed on the heads of the bride and groom, then switched three times. (Prior to the crowning, the crowns sit upon a tray covered with almonds near the altar.) The ceremony usually includes the bride and groom partaking of Communion with a shared cup. Finally, the priest leads the couple as they make three circles around the ceremonial altar, concluding the ceremony.

Jewish Ceremonies

The traditional Jewish wedding ceremony is rich in ancient symbolism. Today, the most familiar branches of American Judaism—Reform, Conservative, Orthodox, and Reconstructionist—typically celebrate slightly different versions of the traditional ceremony, with the more conservative observing the ancient traditions most closely and the less conservative observing some of the traditions, rejecting some, and adapting others to reflect contemporary sensibilities.

Strictly speaking, talmudic law states that only three elements are required in order for a couple to be married within the Jewish tradition. Even the presence of a rabbi is not required; the bride and groom are thought to marry themselves, so a rabbi or other officiant need not officially preside over the ceremony. The requirements are

- ❋ that the groom give something of value to the bride (like a ring) and that she accept his gift.
- ❋ that the groom then speak to the bride the ancient declaration "*Harey at mekuddeshet li b'taba'at zo k'dat Moshe v'Israel*" (in English: "Behold, thou are consecrated unto me with this ring according to the law of Moses and of Israel").

❋ that these acts are witnessed by at least two other
people who are not related to each other or to the
bride or groom.

However, the Jewish wedding ceremony as commonly
practiced in the United States includes a number of other
elements and rituals that the couple may wish to include
in their celebration. Among them are the following:

The *b'deken,* in which the groom raises the bride's veil
and confirms her identity before marrying her (a ritual in
remembrance of Jacob, who accidentally married the
wrong woman because he could not see her through her
veil).

The *chuppah,* a canopy that symbolically represents
the home that the bride and groom will make together,
and which they stand under during the ceremony. The
chuppah traditionally was made of fabric, perhaps a tallis or
prayer shawl, its four corners affixed to poles that were
carried by close friends or family members; today, many
couples select a *chuppah* that is freestanding and ornately
decorated, perhaps with flowers.

The *ketubah,* or marriage contract, which was traditionally signed only by the groom but is now often also
signed by the bride, signifying each partner's promise to
carry out his or her marital obligations; it is also signed by
the two witnesses. The *ketubah* is prepared by the rabbi
and includes the bride's and groom's Hebrew names and
the wedding date according to the Hebrew calendar. It
may be signed and read during the ceremony, or the cou-

ple may choose to sign it in advance of the ceremony, surrounded by their family members, and merely have it read during the ceremony.

The blessings over the wine, where the officiant says a blessing over a glass of wine and first the groom and then the bride takes a sip from the cup. The ceremony often includes a wine blessing before the presentation or exchange of the ring(s) and more in conjunction with the *sheva brachot*, or seven blessings (see following).

The sheva brachot, or seven blessings, which celebrate God's bountiful gifts, including marriage.

The breaking of the glass, in which the groom ritually crushes a glass (which has been wrapped or placed in a cloth pouch) with a stomp of his foot and the guests respond with *"Mazel tov!"* ("Good luck!") There are several interpretations of the symbolism of the breaking of the glass. Many believe that the ritual commemorates the destruction of the Temple in Jerusalem and reminds all gathered that even in moments of joy we must remember the suffering of the past, and that suffering is an ever-present part of life. Some say that it reminds everyone of the fragility of life and love and serves to remind all gathered that the new couple should be supported and protected as they begin their new life together. To others, the breaking of the glass symbolically represents the physical consummation of the marriage.

Protestant Ceremonies

Protestantism today comprises numerous churches with distinct traditions. Generally speaking, however, the Protestant tradition with regard to the wedding ceremony reflects the Catholic roots of Protestantism. As in the Roman Catholic tradition, marriage is a sacrament in the Episcopal tradition, so the wedding celebration is a mass service held within the church. The other major Protestant denominations—Baptist, Lutheran, Methodist, and Presbyterian, among others—do not require that the marriage service be conducted within the physical church itself. Generally speaking, Communion is not a regular part of the marriage celebration, although most Protestant officiants will include it in the service at the request of an observant couple.

Vow Basics

Vow Forms

Wedding vows traditionally take one of several forms, although within a single ceremony multiple forms might be employed. These are the common forms:

- ❀ **Interrogative,** in which the officiant asks questions of the bride and groom (usually one at a time) and they respond with an affirmative "I will" or "I do." The bride's and groom's names and the relative nouns (husband, wife) and pronouns (he, she) are switched between the two recitations.
- ❀ **Directed,** in which the officiant directs the bride and groom to individually repeat phrases after him or her; the officiant essentially "prompts" the lines of the vows to the speaker a few words at a time, the vows having been customized as needed with the correct proper names and pronouns.
- ❀ **Monologue,** in which the bride and groom each recite their vows from memory rather than in response to questions or direction from the officiant.

Among the factors to consider when selecting the form of your vows:

* ❁ What are the vow conventions or restrictions, if any, for a ceremony within your faith or religious institution?

* ❁ Will you be satisfied by a ceremony that simply includes the bride and groom saying "I will" or "I do," or do you want a ceremony where you more explicitly express your commitment? (If you want the latter, you should select vows in the directed or monologue format.)

* ❁ To what degree do you feel you can successfully recite vows from memory, despite your jitters or a possible case of "stage fright," while in the spotlight during your ceremony? (If you think you're likely to go blank in the big moment, you should select vows in an interrogative or directed form.)

* ❁ How important is it to you that the entire congregation hear your vows? In larger ceremony locations, such as churches, synagogues, and hotel ballrooms, the officiant and speakers will be using microphones to make sure all the guests can hear them; will you be comfortable speaking into a microphone? (If you don't want to worry about dealing with a microphone, you will probably want to stick to vows in an interrogative or directed form. Or ask your officiant if he or she can direct a

microphone toward you during your monologue
format vows so your hands will remain free.)

For most couples, the best choice is the directed format—the "middle ground" between vows that are spoken
by the officiant and merely affirmed by the couple and
vows that require the bride and groom to "carry the show."
Work with your officiant to determine which vows are
right for you and will best fit within the entire ceremony.
If you decide to include vows in the monologue format,
be sure that someone who will be close to you during the
ceremony—perhaps the officiant or an attendant—has
a written copy of your vows, in case you forget your lines.
If your officiant is in agreement, you can feel free to combine the different forms within your ceremony.

Traditional Marriage Vows

$\mathcal{F}$or centuries, marrying couples recited the wedding vows of their particular religious or cultural tradition— perhaps without even considering an alternative. It wasn't until the latter half of the twentieth century that the rote recitation of traditional vows came into question and that many couples chose to recite vows of their own creation, in place of traditional vows or in addition to them. Still, most couples find it useful to refer to traditional vows, even if only as a jumping-off point for creating their personal wedding vows.

Religious Vows

Whether or not you wish to be married within a particular religious tradition, whether or not you wish to recite traditional vows or the vows of any particular faith, you may find it helpful to read through this collection of traditional religious wedding vows. Read carefully, noting any words or phrases that stand out to you, that are relevant to you and your relationship. You may decide you want to incorporate particular phrases and expressions into your customized vows. You may find that a religious vow, adapted to remove any explicit religious references, will suit your ceremony plans perfectly. However, take care when adapting traditional vows to ensure that you don't unwittingly show disrespect for the traditions from which you are borrowing.

Here is a summary of the vow traditions for several major religions, denominations, and sects; also noted are religious traditions that do not normally include spoken vows:

Buddhist

The Buddhist ceremony traditionally does not include an exchange of spoken vows.

Eastern Orthodox

In the Eastern Orthodox tradition, the couple's vows are silent; however, one sect of the Eastern Orthodox Church, the Carpatho-Russian Orthodox sect, sometimes includes the spoken expression of these vows:

"I, [speaker's name], take you, [partner's name], as my wedded [wife/husband], and I promise to love, honor, and respect; to be faithful to you; and not to forsake you until death do us part. So help me God, one in the Holy Trinity, and all the Saints."

Episcopal

"I, [speaker's name], take you, [partner's name], to be my wedded [husband/wife], to have and to hold from this day forward, for better, for worse, for richer, for poorer, in sickness and in health, to love and to cherish, till death do us part, according to God's holy ordinance; and thereto I give thee my troth."

Or:

"In the name of God, I, [speaker's name], take you, [partner's name], to be my [wife/husband], to have and to hold, from this day forward, for better, for worse, for richer, for poorer, in sickness and in health, to love and to cherish, until parted by death. This is my solemn vow."

Hindu

The traditional Hindu wedding celebration includes a celebration of the seven steps, which correlate to seven vows on the nature of the marriage commitment. The vows may be recited by the couple, although many couples choose to physically or symbolically represent the vows. Among the vows or steps sometimes recited verbally are these:

"Let us take the fourth step, to acquire knowledge, happiness, and harmony by mutual love and trust. Finally, let us take the seventh step and become true companions and remain lifelong partners by this wedlock."

Interfaith (Ecumenical, Monotheistic)

"[Partner's name], I now take you to be my wedded [wife/husband], to live together after God's ordinance in the holy relationship of marriage. I promise to love and comfort you, honor and keep you, and forsaking all others, I will be yours alone as long as we both shall live."

Jewish

In the traditional Jewish ceremony, the vow of greatest importance is spoken in conjunction with the presentation of the ring. (See "Ring Vows.")

In the Reform wedding service, this wedding vow may also be included, directed toward the groom and the bride, one at a time:

RABBI: "O God, supremely blessed, supreme in might and glory, guide and bless this groom and bride. Standing here in the presence of God, the Guardian of the home, ready to enter into the bond of wedlock, answer in the fear of God, and in the hearing of those assembled: Do you, [partner to whom the rabbi is speaking], of your own free will and consent, take [other partner] to be your [wife/husband], and do you promise to love, honor, and cherish [her/him] throughout life?"

GROOM/BRIDE: "I do."

The *Rabbinical Assembly Manual*, a guide for many Conservative synagogues, provides this vow exchange for the ceremony, which includes the ring vow and is led by the rabbi:

RABBI (to the groom): "Do you, [groom's name], take [bride's name] to be your lawful wedded wife, to love, to honor, and to cherish?"

GROOM: "I do."

RABBI (to the bride): "Do you, [bride's name], take [groom's name] to be your lawful wedded husband, to love, to honor, and to cherish?"

BRIDE: "I do."

RABBI (to the groom): "Then, do you, [groom's name], put this ring upon the finger of your bride and say to her: 'Be thou consecrated to me, as my wife, by this ring, according to the law of Moses and of Israel.'"

The groom repeats the vow as directed by the rabbi. The rabbi then asks the bride to repeat after him this vow: "May this ring I receive from thee be a token of my having become thy wife according to the law of Moses and of Israel." Or, if the bride is presenting the groom with a ring, she may repeat after the rabbi: "This ring is a symbol that thou art my husband in accordance with the law of Moses and of Israel."

In some services the bride or groom may recite vows based on the Song of Songs 7:10: "I am my beloved's, and my beloved is mine."

Lutheran

"I take you, [partner's name], to be my [husband/wife]

from this day forward, to join with you and share all that is to come, and I promise to be faithful to you until death parts us."

Muslim

The traditional Muslim ceremony focuses on the moment when the officiant explains the nature of the bride and groom's commitment to one another, and they acknowledge their consent to be married to one another—not the exchange of vows. However, the Muslim ceremony does traditionally include this exchange:

BRIDE: "I, [bride's name], offer you myself in marriage in accordance with the instructions of the Holy Qur'an and the Holy Prophet, peace and blessing be upon Him. I pledge, in honesty and with sincerity, to be for you an obedient and faithful wife."

GROOM: "I pledge, in honesty and sincerity, to be for you a faithful and helpful husband."

Methodist

"In the Name of God, I, [speaker's name], take you, [partner's name], to be my [husband/wife], to have and to hold, from this day forward, for better, for worse, for richer, for poorer, in sickness and in health, to love and to cherish, until we are parted by death. This is my solemn vow."

Presbyterian

"I, [speaker's name], take you to be my [wife/husband],

and I do promise and covenant, before God and these witnesses, to be your loving and faithful [husband/wife], in plenty and in want, in joy and in sorrow, in sickness and in health, as long as we both shall live."

Protestant

"I, [speaker's name], take thee, [partner's name], to be my wedded [wife/husband], to have and to hold, from this day forward, for better, for worse, for richer, for poorer, in sickness and in health, to love and to cherish, till death do us part, according to God's holy ordinance; and thereto I pledge thee my faith."

Roman Catholic

"I, [speaker's name], take you, [partner's name], for my lawful [wife/husband], to have and to hold, from this day forward, for better, for worse, for richer, for poorer, in sickness and health, until death do us part."

Or:

"I, [speaker's name], take you, [partner's name], to be my [husband/wife]. I promise to be true to you in good times and in bad, in sickness and in health. I will love and honor you all the days of my life."

Quaker

"In the presence of God and these our Friends, I take thee to be my [wife/husband], promising with Divine assistance to be unto thee a loving and faithful [husband/wife] so long as we both shall live."

Unitarian/Universalist

"I, [speaker's name], take you, [partner's name], to be my [wife/husband], to have and to hold, from this day forward, for better, for worse, for richer, for poorer, in sickness and in health, to love and cherish always."

Or, in a more interrogatory version, led by the officiant:

OFFICIANT: "[Partner to whom the officiant is speaking], will you take [other partner] to be your [husband/wife]; will you love, honor, and cherish [him/her] now and forevermore?" The bride and groom in turn answer: "I will."

The officiant then directs the bride and groom to repeat after him (one at a time): "I, [speaker's name], take you, [partner's name], to be my [husband/wife]; to have and to hold from this day forward, for better, for worse, for richer, for poorer, in sickness and in health, to love and cherish always."

The officiant then asks the bride and groom (one at a time): "[Partner to whom the officiant is speaking], will you have [other partner] to be your [husband/wife], to live together in creating an abiding marriage? Will you love and honor, comfort and cherish [him/her], in sickness and in health, in sorrow and in joy, from this day forward?" The bride and groom in turn answer: "I will."

United Church of Christ

"I, [speaker's name], take you, [partner's name], to be my [husband/wife], and I promise to love and sustain you in the bonds of marriage from this day forward, in sickness and in health, in plenty and in want, in joy and in sorrow, till death shall part us, according to God's holy ordinance."

Other Religious Vows

"I, [speaker's name], take you, [partner's name], to be my [wife/husband], and I do so commit myself, before God and this company, to be your loving and faithful [wife/husband]."

"I, [speaker's name], take you, [partner's name], to be my wedded [wife/husband], to have and to hold, from this day forward, for better, for worse, for richer, for poorer, in sickness and in health, to love and to cherish, till death do us part, according to God's holy ordinance, and thereto I pledge you my faith."

"I, [speaker's name], make with you, [partner's name], this covenant of marriage, to live with you according to God's will. I promise to love and trust you, to speak the truth to you, to sustain and nurture you, and with you to receive each day as a gift from God."

Nonreligious Vows

These commonly used nonreligious vows might provide you with ideas, words, and phrases to be incorporated into your personalized vows.

Wedding Vows

Interfaith (Nonreligious)

For an interfaith ceremony, many couples choose to recite vows that combine their specific religious traditions; others prefer to use vows, such as this one, that do not refer to any particular belief or tradition:

OFFICIANT: "I, [speaker's name], take you, [partner's name], to be my [wife/husband]. I promise to be true to you in good times and in bad, in sickness and in health. I will love you and honor you all the days of my life."

Civil Ceremony

OFFICIANT: "I, [Partner's name], take you to be my lawfully wedded [husband/wife]. Before these witnesses I vow to love you and care for you as long as we both shall live. I take you with all your faults and your strengths as I offer myself to you with my faults and strengths. I will help you when you need help, and I will turn to you when I need help. I choose you as the person with whom I will spend my life."

Other Nonreligious Vows

OFFICIANT: "[Bride's name], do you take [groom's name] to be your husband; to live together with him in the covenant of marriage? Do you promise to love him, comfort him, honor and keep him, in sickness and in health; and, forsaking all others, to be faithful unto him as long as you both shall live?"

BRIDE: "I do."

The Basics

OFFICIANT: "[Groom's name], do you take [bride
to be your wife; to live together with her in the co\
of marriage? Do you promise to love her, comfort ⸌ꜱ,
honor and keep her, in sickness and in health; and, forsaking all others, to be faithful unto her as long as you
both shall live?"

GROOM: "I do."

I, _____, take you, _____, to be my wedded [hus-
band/wife], to have and to hold, from this day forward, for
better, for worse, for richer, for poorer, in sickness and in
health, to love and to cherish, till death do us part.

I, _____, take you, _____, to be my [husband/wife],
to have and to hold, from this day forward, for better or for
worse, for richer or for poorer, in sickness and in health, to
love and to cherish as long as we both shall live.

I, _____, take you, _____, to be my [husband/wife].
I faithfully promise to love and support you from this day
forward, in sickness and in health, in plenty and in want,
in success and in failure, in joy and in worry, as long as we
both shall live.

I, _____, take you, _____, to be my [husband/wife],
and in so doing, I commit my life to you, encompassing all
sorrows and joys, all hardships and triumphs, all the expe-
riences of life. A commitment made in love, kept in faith,
lived in hope, and eternally made new.

_____, I give myself to you to be your [husband/wife], and I promise to love and sustain you in the covenant of marriage, from this day forward—in sickness and in health, in plenty and in want, in joy and in sorrow, as long as we both shall live.

_____, I give myself to you to be your [husband/wife], I pledge to share my life openly with you, to speak the truth to you in love. I promise to honor and tenderly care for you, to cherish and encourage your own fulfillment as an individual through all the changes of our lives.

Ring Vows

In many traditional ceremonies, the exchange of vows between the bride and groom continues with the recitation of additional vows during the exchange of rings. Typically, in a double ring ceremony (where the bride and groom each receive a ring), the vow is essentially identical, with merely a switching of the nouns or pronouns as needed; if only the bride is receiving a ring, she of course does not recite the vow. Many religious traditions have a standardized set of vows for the ring exchange.

Episcopal

The groom places the wedding ring on the bride's hand, saying, "[Bride's name], I give you this ring as a symbol of my vow, and with all that I am and all that I have, I honor you, in the name of the Father, and of the Son, and of the Holy spirit." In a double ring ceremony, the priest then blesses the groom's ring, which the bride places on the groom's finger as she recites the same sentence.

Jewish

Before placing the ring on the bride's hand, the groom says, "*Harey at mekuddeshet li b'taba'at zo k'dat Moshe v'Israel*" (in English: "Behold, thou are consecrated unto me with this ring according to the law of Moses and of Israel"). The groom then places the ring on the bride's index finger (most Jewish brides later move the ring to the third finger of the left hand). In traditional Orthodox and some Conservative Jewish ceremonies, the groom does not receive a ring. However, if the groom is to receive a ring, the bride, in like manner, recites the same sentence (adjusted as necessary to reflect the gender difference) and places the groom's ring on his finger.

Presbyterian

The groom places the bride's ring on her finger, saying, "This ring I give you, in token and pledge of our constant faith and abiding love." In a double ring ceremony, the bride then places the groom's ring on his finger and recites the same sentence.

Protestant

The officiant blesses the rings, and then the groom places the ring on the bride's finger, saying, "I give you this ring as a symbol of my love; and with all that I am and all that I have, I honor you, in the name of the Father, and of the Son, and of the Holy Spirit." In a double ring ceremony, the bride then places the groom's ring on his finger and recites the same sentence.

Roman Catholic

The priest blesses the bride's ring, then the groom places it on her finger, saying, "In the name of the Father, the Son, and the Holy Spirit, take and wear this ring as a sign of my love and faithfulness." In a double ring ceremony, the priest then blesses the groom's ring, which the bride places on the groom's finger as she recites the same sentence.

Quaker

Traditionally, the Quaker bride and groom do not exchange rings; hence there are no Quaker ring vows.

Unitarian/Universalist

The groom places the bride's ring on her finger, saying, "With this ring, I wed you, and pledge you my love, now and forever." In a double ring ceremony, the bride then places the groom's ring on his finger and recites the same sentence.

Interfaith Ceremonies

*I*nterfaith ceremonies were once virtually unheard of, but today they are commonplace in the cultural and religious melting pot that is the United States. Still, interfaith marriages meet with unique obstacles. Family members may have objections, and newly engaged couples from different religious backgrounds are often surprised to discover that many officiants refuse to perform inter-faith ceremonies. If you wish to have an interfaith ceremony, be prepared to meet some resistance, but know that it need not have any impact on your happy future as a couple.

What does it mean to have an interfaith ceremony? It means different things to different couples and to their officiants or religious institutions. If the bride and groom are of different religions, that in itself may distinguish the ceremony as being interfaith, regardless of what religions are represented in the ceremony. More often, an interfaith ceremony means a ceremony between a bride and groom of different religions in which the ceremony itself includes elements from both religions, perhaps even presided over by officiants from each faith.

If you wish to have an interfaith ceremony, you need to decide as quickly as possible where that ceremony will occur and what it will consist of. Specifically:

Will you be married in the bride's house of worship, the groom's house of worship, or a nonreligious location? Different religions, and even different houses of worship within a single religion, may have different policies with regard to "hosting" an interfaith ceremony—and the specific policies may change depending on what that other religion is. The only way to know for sure if you can have an interfaith ceremony in a particular house of worship is to ask.

If your goal in creating an interfaith ceremony is to equally represent both your faiths, your selection of where to marry can be complicated. Unless you plan to have two ceremonies or to marry in a secular location, you will have to choose the house of worship of one of your two faiths; and the "other" faith may appear underrepresented. You may wish to make your selection based on which institution is more accommodating of the kind of ceremony you want to have. If picking one religious location over another becomes too much of an obstacle, you may want to consider a secular location, but you will probably want to first check with your potential officiant(s) to make sure he or she will preside in a secular location.

Will you have a ceremony in keeping with the bride's faith, the groom's faith, or elements of both faiths?

Although most couples wish to recognize both their faiths during their ceremony, it is not permissible in every house of worship, nor will every officiant preside over such a ceremony. Your best bet is to determine where your ceremony will take place and who will preside over it, with an eye toward your ceremony wishes; then work with your officiant(s) and institution to create your interfaith ceremony. If having a truly ecumenical ceremony is important to you, you may have to create your interfaith ceremony at a secular site, officiated by a civil authority who is willing to include the elements you want.

Will you be married by an officiant from the bride's faith, an officiant from the groom's faith, or two officiants—one from each faith? Depending on which faiths you wish to blend in your wedding ceremony, you may find that one of your officiants is willing to perform the ceremony. Generally speaking, an officiant will be more willing to officiate a ceremony that includes elements from another faith or co-officiate an interfaith ceremony if the other religion is not perceived as conflicting with his or her own religion's teaching. For example, many Protestant Christian officiants are willing to officiate or co-officiate a Christian-Jewish interfaith ceremony because the Christian faith has its roots in Judaism. On the other hand, many rabbis—especially those of the Orthodox and Conservative branches—are unlikely to agree to participate in a ceremony with Christian elements.

Some couples become discouraged by the obstacles to planning an interfaith ceremony. Take heart. You may find that other interfaith couples who have already been through it can provide a sympathetic ear and good practical advice. It is important that the bride and groom remain unified in their commitment to creating the wedding celebration that's just right for them.

Reconciling
Religious Issues

*I*t's one of *those* topics—right up there with money, politics, and sex: religion.

If you, your beloved, your families, and your close friends are all of the same faith (or are all nonreligious), the matter of religion isn't likely to cause any problems with regard to your wedding plans. However, in a country as diverse as the United States, that sort of unanimity of belief is increasingly rare. Whatever the differences are, and whoever they are between, it can cause friction between parties as the wedding plans are formalized. Here are some suggestions on how to keep the peace when there are religious differences:

If the bride and groom disagree with each other. This is arguably the most complicated scenario. If the bride and groom have not yet been able to come to an understanding on how religious observance (or nonobservance) is going to be dealt with during their marriage, now is the time. If either partner is secretly harboring the conviction that his or her partner can be persuaded to convert in time for the big event, he or she might want to think again;

after all, do you really want your partner for life to adopt your faith just for show? If your religious convictions are different from your partner's, you may find that over time you will grow to a point of consensus. In the meantime, your best course of action is to seek compromise; work together, with your individual officiants, to create a truly balanced interfaith ceremony. Show respect for your partner's views, even if you don't share them, and understanding that being supportive of his or her spiritual life will benefit both of you in the long run.

If family members disagree with the couple. Literature is filled with stories of star-crossed lovers whose parents didn't approve of their choice of partner. Today that still happens, and often the sticking point is religion. While compromise is always a good policy, some lines in the sand can (hopefully) be observed. Simply put: The decision to have a religious (or nonreligious) ceremony, and specifically what kind, should be the couple's alone. If they are mature enough to wed, they are mature enough to make a decision about something this important. This is the ceremony that unites them for life; it is essential that it be authentic to who they are and what they believe. Nothing good can come from the couple reciting words they don't believe, just to please a family member. A couple should be sensitive to the feelings of close family members but in the end must choose to be true to themselves. This can be difficult; a couple may find family members unwilling to participate in or attend the ceremony because of these differences. In particular, parents may seek to drive a wedge between their child and his or her betrothed. The bride and groom must be in consensus and must stand their ground together. If a family member refuses to share in the day, that is his or her choice. Again, compromise where compromise is possible, but be true to yourselves.

If a friend disagrees with the couple. The rules with regard to family members arguably apply. Offer to agree to disagree, and welcome your friend to share in your celebration. If he or she refuses, so be it.

If the officiant(s) or religious institution disagrees with the couple. If you wish to be married by a particular officiant, or within a particular religious institution, you will probably have to "play by their rules." Yes, it's *your* wedding, but as great as your love is, it probably isn't going to change religious traditions that have been passed down for thousands of years. You can certainly suggest a compromise, but if there is no hope of common ground, you are best off moving on; there are other beautiful places to be married, and you may still be able to find an institution or officiant within your preferred tradition who will make the compromises you seek.

Part 2
Personalizing Your Wedding Ceremony

If you are planning to be married within a religious tradition (or traditions), some elements of your wedding ceremony may be predetermined. However, most religious ceremonies, and certainly secular ceremonies, provide couples with the opportunity to personalize the wedding celebration. Those personal touches may take many forms: the choice of ceremony location and how it is decorated; the attire of the bride, groom, and wedding party; the music played and readings delivered during the ceremony; the couple's vows; and the symbols and rites included in the ceremony.

But what choices are right for you? The following worksheets on personalizing your wedding will help you begin to define the elements that will transform your wedding into a truly personal event.

The Personalization
Worksheets

These worksheets are designed to help you begin to identify the unique aspects of your personality and the things
that are most important to you, that define you as people.
Identifying these elements can help you create a wedding
theme or style that reflects each of you as individuals and
the two of you as a couple. You may wish to shape each
element of your wedding—from the flowers to the readings to the vows—to reflect your personalities.

If you find yourself having difficulty filling out the
forms—if you're unable to identify your favorite composers or don't know what historical period you might
have liked to live in, you might want to set aside some
time over the next few weeks to build a scrapbook of ideas.
Collect images from magazines and copies of poems and
readings that you like. Jot down song titles and lyrics, anything that elicits a strong, positive emotional reaction.
Rent some of your favorite movies—whether they include
wedding scenes or not, whether they are romances or
not—and make notes about what it is you love—the
setting, the time period, the costumes? None of these

elements need be explicitly "wedding related"—you're simply looking to compile a collection of things you like. Review your scrapbook, then revisit your worksheet and see if you aren't better able to articulate the kind of music and writing, the eras and styles, that appeal most to you.

After filling out the worksheets individually, you and your betrothed should sit down and show each other what you've written. You may want to go into greater detail about some items—explaining your choices and so on.

Listen to your partner's answers with an open mind. The worksheet is merely a tool to foster your conversation, it isn't a document that will be set in stone. Sometimes a partner will panic after seeing what his or her intended has written; just because your future spouse lists graduating from Ohio State University as one of his or her proudest accomplishments doesn't mean he or she is going to insist you walk down the aisle to the school's fight song.

As you read through the worksheet answers, note any patterns or like interests that emerge. Does he love Dickens, and do you dream of living in London? (Perhaps a formal, Victorian-influenced wedding, with period attire and music, will be the perfect, unique ceremony for you.) Do you share a love of the outdoors and a passion for nature conservation? (You might want to consider an outdoor ceremony, with readings from Henry David Thoreau's *Walden*, the bride carrying a simple, hand-tied bouquet of wildflowers.) Did you meet in a class on Renaissance literature, and was your first date a festival performance of Shakespeare's *Romeo and Juliet*? (You may want to punctuate your ceremony with readings from the Bard's sonnets.)

As you review your worksheets, you should also note how each of you has rated your interest in a formal or informal wedding, a very spiritual or not very spiritual ceremony, and so forth. In categories where you have a consensus, you have a clear indication of what your ceremony should be. In categories where you do not have a consensus, you should each talk about the selection you made. Look for compromise, and if all else fails, agree to "split the difference" and plan to position that element of your ceremony in the middle ground.

Personalizing Our Wedding— Bride's Worksheet

This worksheet will help you begin to identify aspects of your personality and interests that you may want to inject into your ceremony to create a more personalized event. It also includes questions designed to help you think about what kind of ceremony you might want and what elements it might include. Remember, there are no wrong answers. Be honest, and ask your betrothed to do the same as he fills out the Groom's Worksheet.

The five roles I play in my life that are most important to me are (example: future wife, advertising director, runner, daughter/sister, literacy volunteer, traveler, gardener . . .):

1._____

2._____

3._____

4._____

5._____

The five things in my life that I'm proudest of are:

1._____

2._____

3._____

4._____

5._____

My five favorite hobbies/interests are:

1._____

2._____

3._____

4._____

5._____

My five favorite writers/poems/plays/books are:

1._____

2._____

3._____

4._____

5._____

My five favorite love songs/recording artists/composi-
tions/composers are:

1._____

2._____

3._____

4._____

5._____

If I could go anywhere in the world on vacation, I would like to go _____

If I could live anywhere in the world, I would like to live

_____

If I could have lived in another era, I would like to have lived in _____

If I could have known anyone in history, I would like to have known _____

The best wedding ceremony I've ever witnessed was

_____

The things that made that wedding ceremony wonderful are:

1. _____

2. _____

3. _____

4. _____

5. _____

My five favorite things about my future husband are:

1. _____

2._____

3._____

4._____

5._____

On a scale of 1 to 10 (1 = lowest, 10 = highest), rate what you would like your wedding to be like in each of these categories:

Traditional   1   2   3   4   5   6   7   8   9   10

Formal   1   2   3   4   5   6   7   8   9   10

Spiritual/religious
                 1   2   3   4   5   6   7   8   9   10

Length of ceremony
                 1   2   3   4   5   6   7   8   9   10

Inclusion of family and friends
                 1   2   3   4   5   6   7   8   9   10

Inclusion of readings
                 1   2   3   4   5   6   7   8   9   10

Inclusion of music
                 1   2   3   4   5   6   7   8   9   10

The five elements of the ceremony that are most important to me are:

1. _____

2. _____

3. _____

4. _____

5. _____

The five adjectives I would like people to use to describe our wedding are:

1. _____

2. _____

3. _____

4. _____

5. _____

The five adjectives I *do not* want people to use to describe our wedding are:

1. _____

2._____

3._____

4._____

5._____

My biggest hope for our wedding ceremony is _____

_____

_____

My biggest fear about our wedding ceremony is _____

_____

_____

Personalizing Our Wedding—
Groom's Worksheet

This worksheet will help you begin to identify aspects of your personality and interests that you may want to inject into your ceremony to create a more personalized event. It also includes questions designed to help you think about what kind of ceremony you might want and what elements it might include. Remember, there are no wrong answers. Be honest, and ask your betrothed to do the same as she fills out the Bride's Worksheet.

The five roles I play in my life that are most important to me are (example: future husband, advertising director, runner, son/brother, literacy volunteer, traveler, gardener . . .):

1._____

2._____

3._____

4._____

5._____

The five things in my life that I'm proudest of are:

1._____

2._____

3._____

4._____

5._____

My five favorite hobbies/interests are:

1._____
2._____
3._____
4._____
5._____

My five favorite writers/poems/plays/books are:

1._____
2._____
3._____
4._____
5._____

My five favorite love songs/recording artists/compositions/composers are:

1._____
2._____
3._____

4._____

5._____

If I could go anywhere in the world on vacation, I would like to go _____

If I could live anywhere in the world, I would like to live

_____

If I could have lived in another era, I would like to have lived in _____

If I could have known anyone in history, I would like to have known _____

The best wedding ceremony I've ever witnessed was

_____

The things that made that wedding ceremony wonderful are:

1._____

2._____

3._____

4._____

5._____

My five favorite things about my future wife are:

1._____

2._____

3._____

4._____

5._____

On a scale of 1 to 10 (1 = lowest, 10 = highest), rate what you would like your wedding to be like in each of these categories:

Traditional   1   2   3   4   5   6   7   8   9   10

Formal   1   2   3   4   5   6   7   8   9   10

Spiritual/religious
                1   2   3   4   5   6   7   8   9   10

Length of ceremony
                1   2   3   4   5   6   7   8   9   10

Inclusion of family and friends
                1   2   3   4   5   6   7   8   9   10

Inclusion of readings

     1   2   3   4   5   6   7   8   9   10

Inclusion of music

     1   2   3   4   5   6   7   8   9   10

The five elements of the ceremony that are most important to me are:

1._____

2._____

3._____

4._____

5._____

The five adjectives I would like people to use to describe our wedding are:

1._____

2._____

3._____

4._____

5._____

The five adjectives I *do not* want people to use to describe our wedding are:

1._____

2._____

3._____

4._____

5._____

My biggest hope for our wedding ceremony is _____

_____

_____

My biggest fear about our wedding ceremony is _____

_____

_____

Developing a Theme
for Your Ceremony

*W*hen reviewing the worksheets, you may realize that your shared interests paint a clear picture of a theme or style you want to employ to personalize your wedding ceremony. What is a ceremony theme? It doesn't refer to theme music, although music might be a part of what creates your wedding theme. And before you become worried about this whole matter, rest assured, you aren't required to have a wedding theme.

Simply put, a wedding theme is the style or aesthetic that unifies the event. You may already have selected one without realizing it.

If you plan to wear cowboy boots and a Stetson with your tuxedo, your bride is carrying the yellow roses of Texas, and your reception will be a barbecue held on Big Daddy's palatial spread, you may have created a western theme to your wedding (even if you didn't realize it). If you're marrying at the Waldorf-Astoria Hotel in New York City, the bride is wearing a vintage sheath gown, and the reception will include classic jazz and a martini bar, you're arguably planning a 1920s or Gatsby theme wedding.

There's no right or wrong way to arrive at the selection of your wedding theme. You can select a theme and then determine the elements that will define it or start with a few elements that are interesting or important to you and develop a theme from there. The Personalization Worksheets can help you define a theme by starting with your interests and preferences.

Clearly, one of the best reasons to create a theme for your wedding is to personalize the event, to make it reflect who you are as individuals and as a couple, and to make the event unique—not just another wedding. It can also act to unify the event, to hold the various elements together, if that is your desire. If you're stuck making choices—what kind of cake, how it should be decorated, what to give as favors—your wedding theme can help narrow the choices and define the elements.

In earlier decades the selection of a theme impacted the reception far more than the ceremony, as ceremonies were more often "by the book" and shaped largely by the practices of the religious institution where the ceremony was held. Today there is more flexibility, and many couples select elements for their ceremonies that express their event theme. Some are even creating two distinct themes—one for the ceremony and another for the reception.

Many of the most popular wedding themes today are centered around a particular type of geography—the big-city wedding, the country wedding, the seaside wedding—or the time of year—the Christmas wedding, the spring garden wedding, a New Year's Eve wedding celebration. If you've merely selected the date and the location, you may already have the defining elements of your wedding theme. Other themes reflect the fashions and flavors of bygone eras: the Renaissance theme wedding, the Victorian wedding, the Gatsby theme wedding. Your shared religious or cultural heritage, or the combination of elements from each of your backgrounds, might create a wedding theme that uniquely reflects you and your partner and your families.

The wedding theme can most obviously impact your wedding ceremony in the selection of the visual elements: the flowers you will carry and that will decorate the ceremony location; the attire you will wear for the ceremony; and so forth. However, if you have embraced a theme for your wedding, you may wish to play upon your theme with the specific elements of your ceremony—your vows, your readings, the musical selections.

For example: If you are creating a wedding that celebrates your shared African heritage, you may wish to flavor your ceremony with readings about love from celebrated African American writers such as Maya Angelou and Toni Morrison and include traditions such as the jumping the broom rite. If you both love the ocean and are planning a seaside wedding, you may want to include readings from Anne Morrow Lindbergh's *A Gift from the Sea*; read your vows from scrolls of paper which you can then commingle in a bottle, cork, and cast into the sea—a message of love sent to unknown parts beyond. (Just make sure you aren't violating any environmental laws!)

Your worksheets thus become the jumping-off point for creating your wedding theme. Keep in mind that your theme can be subtle—expressed through just a few details such as the flowers, the vows, and the readings—or it can define every element of your ceremony, from the attire and flowers to the readings, rites, and music. You may want to use the Theme Worksheet below to define your theme and its elements.

Theme Worksheet

Wedding date, time, and season: _____

Wedding location: _____

Geographical features of location: _____

_____

Formality: Informal   Semiformal   Formal

Religious/spiritual elements: _____

_____

_____

Cultural Elements

   From the bride's heritage: _____

_____

Wedding Vows

From the groom's heritage: _____

_____

_____

_____

Attire Ideas

Bride: _____

_____

Groom: _____

_____

Bridesmaids: _____

_____

Groomsmen: _____

_____

Other: _____

_____

Decorating Ideas

Flowers: _____

_____

Religious symbols: _____

_____

Cultural symbols: _____

_____

Family symbols: _____

_____

Other: _____

_____

Thematic readings ideas: _____

_____

_____

_____

_____

Thematic music ideas: _____

_____

_____

_____

_____

Incorporating
Traditions

*I*f you wish to create a ceremony that is filled with meaningful tradition and yet truly personal, you might want to start by reacquainting yourself with the traditions—cultural, religious, or those that have sprung from generations of family practice—that have been a part of your life . . . and that of your future spouse. By selecting among these traditions and combining them in the way that best represents the two of you as a couple, you can create a ceremony that is both traditional and original. You may find the Traditions Worksheets on pages 107 and 110 helpful in organizing and documenting your exploration.

Spend some time with your parents, grandparents, and other family members. Searching out these traditions is in many ways like discovering your roots, your family genealogy, your cultural heritage. Review old wedding photographs and note the details of the weddings of your parents, grandparents, and earlier relatives: What kind of flowers did the bride carry? What was her "old, new, borrowed, and blue"? What did the groom wear? What religious or cultural customs did they incorporate into their ceremony? What were the vows that your parents or grandparents made on their wedding days?

You may want to do some additional research to find out about other religious or cultural traditions you can incorporate to celebrate your heritage.

Some traditions you may want to incorporate exactly as they are practiced by your parents or grandparents. Others you may want to adapt to make more inclusive or egalitarian or to better facilitate the combination of the bride's traditions and the groom's. You should exercise caution if you plan to update a tradition—especially a religious tradition. Some guests may misunderstand your intentions and think that by "rewriting" a tradition, you are tacitly suggesting that as commonly practiced it is somehow flawed. When incorporating traditions, be judicious and make sure you are showing respect for the tradition, even if you aren't following its customary practice. You may want to seek the feedback of an open-minded relative from an older generation to keep you from going too far in updating a tradition.

Traditions—
Bride's Worksheet

Cultural Heritage

Bride's birthplace: _____

Mother's birthplace: _____

Father's birthplace: _____

Maternal grandmother's birthplace: _____

Maternal grandfather's birthplace: _____

Paternal grandmother's birthplace: _____

Paternal grandfather's birthplace: _____

Countries of origin of great-grandparents and earlier

relatives: _____

_____

Other notes on family ancestry and cultural traditions:

_____

_____

Religious Heritage

Bride's religion: _____

Mother's religion: _____

Father's religion: _____

Maternal grandmother's religion: _____

Maternal grandfather's religion: _____

Paternal grandmother's religion: _____

Paternal grandfather's religion: _____

Religions of great-grandparents and earlier relatives:

_____

_____

Other notes on family religious traditions:

_____

_____

Family Traditions

Bride's family's wedding traditions: _____

_____

Distinguishing elements of bride's parents' wedding: _____

_____

Distinguishing elements of bride's maternal grandparents'

wedding: _____

_____

Distinguishing elements of bride's paternal grandparents'

wedding: _____

_____

Traditions—
Groom's Worksheet

Cultural Heritage

Groom's birthplace: _____

Mother's birthplace: _____

Father's birthplace: _____

Maternal grandmother's birthplace: _____

Maternal grandfather's birthplace: _____

Paternal grandmother's birthplace: _____

Paternal grandfather's birthplace: _____

Countries of origin of great-grandparents and earlier

relatives: _____

_____

Other notes on family ancestry and cultural traditions:

_____

Religious Heritage

Groom's religion: _____

Mother's religion: _____

Father's religion: _____

Maternal grandmother's religion: _____

Maternal grandfather's religion: _____

Paternal grandmother's religion: _____

Paternal grandfather's religion: _____

Religions of great-grandparents and earlier relatives:

_____

Other notes on family religious traditions:

_____

_____

Family Traditions

Groom's family's wedding traditions: _____

_____

Distinguishing elements of groom's parents' wedding:

_____

Distinguishing elements of groom's maternal grandparents' wedding: _____

_____

Distinguishing elements of groom's paternal grandparents' wedding: _____

_____

_____

Readings

The tradition of including readings in a wedding ceremony is thought to have originated in religious ceremonies, in which the readings were taken from holy writings or the institution's official wedding liturgy. Today, however, many couples are including nonreligious writings as a part of their ceremony—whether the ceremony itself is religious or secular. Readings are a great way to personalize your ceremony and, if you are so inclined, to extend the expression of your personal wedding theme. Readings can speak to your personalities as individuals or as a couple, or they can reflect your thoughts and feelings about life, love, marriage, and family. Readings are most often delivered by a close friend or family member, so they also become a way to involve those closest to you in the ceremony.

Getting Started

Your first step in selecting readings should be to clarify with your officiant whether or not there are any restrictions with regard to the selection of ceremony readings.

Some religious institutions allow the inclusion of readings only from the religion's scriptures or holy writings. Others may approve of nonreligious readings in combination with religious readings, or they may not require any religious readings at all. In civil ceremonies, readings typically may come from any source.

Next, working from your officiant's direction, you should decide how many readings you want to include in your ceremony. Although there are no real rules about how many readings you can or can't have (unless indicated by your officiant), you will probably want to have between two and four readings. Readings traditionally occur during the first half of the wedding ceremony. They can help create the mood, put the wedding party and guests in a contemplative or celebratory state of mind, and set the stage for the exchange of vows to follow.

What Kinds of Readings?

The only thing a reading need be to "qualify" as appropriate for your wedding is that you really love it. Readings can come from any source: religious scripture, poetry, prose, even song lyrics or your personal love letters. You may want to select readings that extend your wedding theme. For example: If your wedding is a celebration of romance, with lavish floral decorations and candlelight, you might want to select readings from the love poetry of Robert Browning and Elizabeth Barrett Browning.

If there is a piece of writing or a song lyric that you particularly love, read it aloud yourself and make sure it is as powerful when read aloud as it is when read or when sung in a song. Contemporary song lyrics in particular sometimes do not read well, because of the frequent repetition of short phrases. Make sure your readings are as effective when read as they are in their originally intended forms.

There are no "official" limits on the length of a reading, but you will probably want to select something that can be read in under two minutes; it sounds short, but in the midst of a wedding ceremony, it will feel like a lifetime. One to one and a half minutes is an ideal length (approximately 150–250 words). As you evaluate readings, speak them aloud yourself and time your reading. Note reading lengths, so you can refer to them as you narrow down the possibilities, as well as the title and writer/source for each piece, so your reader can identify the reading aloud and/or you can include identifying information in your wedding program, if you so choose.

As you consider readings, keep in mind the people you plan to have deliver them. If your ten-year-old brother is going to do a reading, be sure to select one that contains a vocabulary he can handle, with words he won't stumble over.

Practical Matters

Once you have selected your readings, you will want to determine their order and placement in the wedding service. Your officiant can usually provide good advice with regard to this matter. You will probably want to order and place your readings so that each will occur in the most tonally appropriate place. For example, if you plan to have three readings—one on friendship, one on romance, and one on love—you will probably want to put them in that order, since the progression mimics the deepening of feelings and commitment represented by each kind of relationship.

Match your readers to the readings. Only you can know who might most appropriately deliver each reading. Or, if you are so inclined, approach the reader you are closest to and give that person his or her pick of the readings. (Be careful, though; your other readers may find out, and hurt feelings may result.) Alternatively, if you prefer, you can select your readers first and ask them to select the reading they would like to deliver, as an expression of their friendship and love. Most readers would prefer that you select the readings you want, but some will appreciate the opportunity to play a more instrumental role in creating your wedding celebration.

If a reader tells you that he or she is uncomfortable with the reading, try to get to the root of the dissatisfaction. Perhaps you can switch his or her reading with that of another reader.

Provide each reader with his or her reading in writing at least two weeks in advance of the ceremony, and make several backup copies. Bring one extra copy to the rehearsal and have another ready for the big day, just in case. Your readers will probably find it more helpful if you have the readings typed in a large typeface, double spaced, and adhered to notecards. If there are any tricky pronunciations, provide your reader with a phonetic key.

Popular Readings and Writers

Among the most popular religious readings are these from the Hebrew and Christian Bibles:

Genesis 2:12–24 (the story of Creation)

Song of Songs 7:10 ("I am my beloved's, and my beloved is mine")

Ruth 1:16–17 (a pledge of devotion and solidarity)

Matthew 19:5–6 (". . . a man shall leave his father and mother and cleave to his wife . . .")

John 4:7–16 (on the nature of love and of God's love for man)

I Corinthians 13:1–13 (a well-known passage on the nature of love)

Popular secular readings include those taken from the works of Walt Whitman, Emily Dickinson, William Butler Yeats, Percy Bysshe Shelley, e. e. cummings, Pablo Neruda, John Donne, Kahlil Gibran, Robert Frost, William Carlos Williams, Maya Angelou, Rainer Maria Rilke, John Keats, William Shakespeare (Sonnet 18: "Shall I compare thee to a summer's day?"), and Elizabeth Barrett Browning (*Sonnets from the Portuguese*, Sonnet XLIII: "How do I love thee? Let me count the ways . . .").

Incorporating a Reading into Your Vows

If there is a piece of writing that you are particularly fond of and that perfectly expresses your feelings for your intended, you might want to consider incorporating it into your personal vows. Readings that are in the first person (as if a person is speaking, "I hear your voice . . .") are sometimes not well suited for traditional readings, because it appears that the reader is speaking of his or her love for some unknown person. These kinds of expressions might better be included within your personal vows, especially if you plan to deliver them in a monologue format. Be sure to indicate, by mentioning the source, the work you are quoting, so your guests won't be puzzled that a portion of your vows sounds so familiar. For example, you might say, "Our favorite writer, the great W. B. Yeats, put it best in his poem 'When You Are Old' when he wrote, '. . . one man loved the pilgrim soul in you. . . .'"

Readings Worksheet

Readings Ideas

	Title	Writer/Source	Reading Length

Religious: _____

_____

_____

Wedding Vows

	Title	Writer/Source	Reading Length

Cultural: _____

_____

_____

Thematic: _____

_____

_____

Poetry: _____

_____

_____

Prose: _____

_____

_____

Song lyrics: _____

_____

_____

Other: _____

_____

_____

Reader   **Reading Selected**

_____   _____

_____   _____

_____   _____

_____   _____

_____   _____

_____   _____

Music

$\mathcal{M}$usic is an essential part of any wedding ceremony. And music can do more than just create a backdrop for the event. In addition to the most familiar musical elements of the wedding ceremony—the processional and recessional—most weddings include at least one or two musical selections during the ceremony, as well as music during the seating of the guests, before the ceremony. Your selection of music—whether sacred or secular, whether strictly instrumental or including a vocal performance— adds to your ceremony much as readings do. Music can evoke your wedding theme or celebrate your cultural heritage. And live music in particular simply brings things to life.

Getting Started

Be sure to check with your officiant and ceremony location to find out what restrictions, if any, there are with regard to ceremony music. Some houses of worship will permit instrumental music only; a few forbid instruments, and only singing is allowed. You should also find out what equipment might be provided—sound equipment, a piano or pipe organ? Find out if there are rules about who can operate the equipment or play the on-site instruments. The house of worship might have a resident musician who can fill your music needs perfectly—he or she will probably be less expensive than an outside performer, and you have the added benefit of using an experienced musician who knows the equipment and the acoustics of the location.

You should also consult your budget. If you are not accustomed to hiring professional musicians, you might be surprised at the cost, and each additional instrument means a bigger price tag. Don't worry: You can have a rich musical offering with just a single musician. Whether you select a piano or pipe organ, a guitarist or harpist, you can have beautiful ceremony music without hiring a thirty-piece orchestra. If you still need to cut corners, consider hiring a musician who can provide music for both your ceremony and your reception (for example, find out if the keyboardist who will be playing with the jazz combo at your reception can also play traditional organ music at your ceremony); you may get a break on costs for the extended booking.

What Kind of Music?

Beyond any restrictions made by your ceremony location or officiant, you really can feel free to select whatever music you want for your ceremony. Generally speaking, couples opt for music that is traditional and somewhat "serious," but there's no reason you can't walk down the aisle to your favorite pop ballad.

As you begin to evaluate possible ceremony music, there are a number of matters you might want to take into consideration. Do you want ceremony music that extends your wedding theme by selecting music from a particular culture or era? Would you like to honor your parents by including musical selections that were performed at their weddings? Do you want to create a contrast between your ceremony music and your reception music? How important to you is it that the music performed at your ceremony be familiar to your guests? (If it is important, you should select well-known melodies.) If you pick an unusual kind of music or unusual songs, do you risk having trouble finding someone to perform at your ceremony?

By picking the music you love, that is important to you, you instantly personalize your ceremony. However, don't let your love for a piece of music get the best of you. As much as you may love that new pop song that has become "your song," it may seem out of place during your ceremony; save it for your reception instead, possibly for your first dance. Also, keep in mind that a song you love when performed by a professional orchestra or string ensemble may not work when played on the piano or a single guitar. You should develop your music ideas before you interview musicians, but be prepared to work with the musician(s) you eventually select to get the best results. You will probably want to list your musical selections by title and composer in your wedding program and may also want to note the significance of each selection.

Although the vast majority of ceremony music is performed live, some weddings do feature recorded music for the ceremony. If your budget is tight, this might be a way to cut a corner, but hiring someone to come in and push the buttons might not be any less expensive than having one talented musician. If you love recorded popular music, you can incorporate it in your celebration, but you might want to save it for the reception instead.

If your ceremony is to follow the most common format, it will include several musical selections that serve a particular function in the structure of the ceremony and thus have a fairly defined place in the proceedings; other selections may occur during the service at your discretion (much like the readings). Traditional musical elements include the following:

❈ **The prelude** (which may be more than one piece of music performed consecutively) is the music played before the ceremony begins, as guests are entering and being seated. Music selected for the prelude tends to be rather soft and serious, particularly for a religious ceremony, allowing guests to tune out the distractions of the outside world and become in an attitude of prayer. The prelude typically starts about thirty minutes before the ceremony is

scheduled to begin. It concludes just before the ceremony begins, after the final honored guest/family
member is seated.

✤ **The processional** is the music that begins after the
prelude, just after the final family member is seated
(in Christian weddings this is typically the mother
of the bride, who is the last honored guest to be
escorted down the aisle before the ceremony
begins). Today many couples actually select two
songs for the processional: one for the entrance of
the wedding party and another for the bride's
entrance. The processional pieces tend to be somewhat slow and dramatic—after all, this is the
music to which the wedding party will be walking
down the aisle. The second of the two pieces
might begin with a bit of fanfare to "announce"
the entrance of the bride.

✤ **The recessional** is the music that plays at the end
of the ceremony, as the bride and groom, and then
their attendants, walk back up the aisle. It tends to
be rather lively in tempo and somewhat celebratory.

As already mentioned, many wedding ceremonies
include an additional musical selection or two; often one
of these features a vocal soloist. These typically occur during the first half of the ceremony, perhaps interspersed
with the readings, although many couples place a musical
selection toward the end of the ceremony, after the
exchange of rings but before the pronouncement, during

which the couple may participate in lighting a unity candle or present roses to their mothers.

Practical Matters

❀ Don't hire a musician you have not heard perform live. Most musicians who perform for weddings can provide you with a tape of their work, but you want to hear them live to make sure they haven't "sweetened" the recording to make them sound better than they really are.

❀ If you hire through an agency, or if you are hiring a group of musicians through a manager or band leader, make sure that the musicians you have seen perform live and like are the same ones who will be performing at your ceremony; you don't want to end up with the "understudies."

❀ Make sure there is an explicit understanding of when the musicians are expected to arrive, when the ceremony is scheduled to begin and conclude, and how the performers will be attired.

❀ If a musician, manager, or agent tells you that your request for a certain song can't be fulfilled, take them at their word and don't try to convince them to play something they can't. They are professionals, and if they say it's not possible, it isn't. You really don't want them to try and fail on your special day.

❈ Your musicians will probably not be at your rehearsal. Make sure they are familiar with the ceremony location and have spoken to the location coordinator about microphones and the like, or, if they are willing, ask that they visit the location with you in advance of the wedding to check out the facilities.

Popular Musical Selections and Composers

Among the most popular musical selections and composers for ceremony music are these pieces:

"Bridal Chorus" (from *Lohengrin*) by Wagner
"Wedding March" (from *A Midsummer Night's Dream*) by Mendelssohn
Canon in D by Pachelbel
"Hallelujah Chorus" by Handel
"Trumpet Aire in C" by Purcell
"Autumn" and "Spring" (from *The Four Seasons*) by Vivaldi
"Let the Bright Seraphim" by Handel
"Water Music" (various selections) by Handel
Allegro by Vivaldi
Allegro in G Minor by Albinoni
"Jesu, Joy of Man's Desiring" by Bach
"Ave Maria" by Shubert
"The Wedding Song" by Paul Stookey

Incorporating Song Lyrics into Your Vows

For some couples, the lyrics of a favorite song are so special and meaningful that they are the perfect words for their wedding vows. As discussed in the section on readings, you should feel free to incorporate a song lyric into your personal vows (again, presuming that this has been approved by your officiant). You should probably plan to indicate the source of the words before you deliver them ("And what really sums it up best are the lines from our favorite song, 'You've Got a Friend,' by James Taylor, when he says . . ."), so guests won't think that you're trying to pull a fast one with your beautiful "borrowed" words.

Music Worksheet

Music Ideas

Title	Composer/Source	To Be Performed By

Religious: _____

_____

_____

Cultural: _____

_____

_____

Thematic: _____

_____

_____

Traditional: _____

_____

_____

Contemporary: _____

_____

_____

Other: _____

_____

_____

Placement in Ceremony   **Musical Selection**

_____   _____

_____   _____

_____   _____

_____   _____

_____   _____

Writing Your Vows

*A*fter discussing the options with your officiant, you may decide that personally written vows are the best way for you to express your commitment to one another. Depending on the circumstances of your ceremony, you may wish to deliver your personal vows as the sole vows of the ceremony or in addition to more traditional marriage vows.

The idea of delivering vows you have written yourself—that personally express your feelings about your partner—is appealing to many couples; it's sitting down and writing them that can be difficult. The information and worksheets in this section will help you sort through your thoughts and feelings and begin to put on paper the words and phrases that will become your wedding vows. Don't put off working on your vows until the final days before your wedding. Your marriage vows are arguably the most important words you will ever speak. Especially if you are writing your own vows, you want them to be authentic to who you and your partner are and to the nature of your relationship and your commitment to one another.

Getting Started

There's no right or wrong way to write your vows; whatever process allows you to generate the desired output—wonderful vows that really express what's in your heart—is the right way for you.

You will probably want to start by defining the basic parameters of your vows (probably in consultation with your officiant)—when the vows will occur in the ceremony, approximately how long they will be, and how they will be delivered. Most couples then choose to work individually on their vows. Your officiant will probably be able to provide useful guidance in writing your vows, whether you consult with him or her as a couple or individually. If your personally written vows will be delivered in conjunction with other, traditional vows, be sure to consider the substance of those preset vows before you write your own; you don't want to end up saying the same things twice. You may decide that you want to create a contrast between the traditional or preset vows and your personal vows; for example, if the traditional vows are serious, you might want your personal vows to be a little more lighthearted.

As you set out to write your vows, take some time to think deeply about what your partner and what this important commitment mean to you. If you keep a journal or have letters you have exchanged, set aside a few hours to reread them.

Among the questions you may want to consider as you begin to shape your vows:

❋ How do you feel about marriage in general? Why is the decision to get married personally important to you? Your answer may be connected to your feelings about your own parents, their marriage, your childhood, and so forth.

❋ Why have you chosen this person to share your life with? What unique qualities does he or she have, and why are those traits important to you? What aspects of your partner's character and values do you treasure most, and why?

❋ How has your partner changed your life? How do you hope to positively influence his or her life?

❋ What do you bring to this union, in terms of feelings, beliefs, needs, desires, hopes, fears, and dreams?

❋ What does your partner bring to this union, in terms of feelings, beliefs, needs, desires, hopes, fears, and dreams?

❋ What do you imagine your lives will be like ten, twenty-five, and even fifty years in the future?

❋ If you and your partner plan to have children, how do you feel about building a family with this person?

The Vow Ideas Worksheets on pages 132 and 136 will help you begin to organize your thoughts about your wedding vows.

Vow Ideas—
Bride's Worksheet

What I remember most about

. . . the first moment I saw him: _____

_____

_____

_____

. . . the first thing he said to me/I said to him: _____

_____

_____

_____

. . . our first kiss: _____

_____

_____

_____

. . . the moment when I realized I loved him: _____

_____

_____

_____

. . . when we decided to marry: _____

_____

_____

_____

Lyrics/quotes that reflect how I feel about him:

Phrase   **Song/Source/Writer**

_____

_____

_____

_____

_____

_____

_____

_____

_____

_____

_____

My favorite things about him: _____

_____

_____

Wedding Vows

The amazing thing about him that no one knows is:

_____

_____

_____

Things I promise to do/be for my future husband: _____

_____

_____

_____

Some of the wonderful things he has done for me: _____

_____

_____

_____

The ways I have changed for the better since he came into my life: _____

_____

_____

_____

How I imagine our lives will be in 10, 25, and even 50 years: _____

_____

_____

_____

The three most important things about marriage are:

1. _____

_____

2. _____

_____

3. _____

_____

The three things I most want him to know on our wedding day are:

1. _____

_____

2. _____

_____

3. _____

_____

Vow Ideas—
Groom's Worksheet

What I remember most about

. . . the first moment I saw her: _____

_____

_____

_____

. . . the first thing she said to me/I said to her: _____

_____

_____

_____

. . . our first kiss: _____

_____

_____

_____

. . . the moment when I realized I loved her: _____

_____

_____

_____

. . . when we decided to marry: _____

_____

_____

_____

Lyrics/quotes that reflect how I feel about her:

Phrase   **Song/Source/Writer**

_____

_____

_____

_____

_____

_____

_____

_____

_____

_____

_____

_____

Wedding Vows

My favorite things about her: _____

_____

_____

_____

The amazing thing about her that no one knows is:

_____

_____

_____

Things I promise to do/be for my future wife: _____

_____

_____

_____

Some of the wonderful things she has done for me:

_____

_____

_____

The ways I have changed for the better since she came
into my life: _____

_____

_____

_____

How I imagine our lives will be in 10, 25, and even 50 years: _____

_____

_____

_____

The three most important things about marriage are:

1. _____

_____

2. _____

_____

3. _____

_____

The three things I most want her to know on our wedding day are:

1. _____

_____

2. _____

_____

3. _____

_____

Vow Sources

You may decide that the words and phrases that con-stitute your wedding vows—or parts of them—will be drawn from existing sources. Including a line or two from another source doesn't make your vows any less personal; rather, the "personal" aspect of your vows comes through in your individual decision to include those elements, because they so effectively express your sentiments. The potential sources are endless; among them are the following:

- ❋ poetry, whether by a master or of your own composition
- ❋ prose, including religious texts or writings from your cultural background
- ❋ song lyrics (especially if it is "your song," a song you both love, even a song that will be included in your ceremony or used for your first dance)
- ❋ your letters to one another
- ❋ your letters to or from family members or friends about your new love
- ❋ the vows spoken by your parents or grandparents
- ❋ other established wedding vows (see "Traditional Marriage Vows," page 59)

Generally speaking, you can feel free to use lines from any of these sources, but always exercise common sense in doing so; don't quote from a personal letter without the permission of the writer, and exercise care if "borrowing" or rewriting vows from religious traditions you don't observe. If you desire to include a line from a published piece of writing or music, you will probably want to indicate the source so everyone will understand that you're quoting a well-known source and not just borrowing someone else's words.

You may want to tie the substance of your vows to your larger ceremony theme or elements. Revisit the Theme Worksheet (page 103), Traditions Worksheets (pages 107 and 110), Readings Worksheet (page 117), and Music Worksheet (page 127). You might extend the theme of your wedding within your vows by using lines from thematically relevant music or writings. A single profound line repurposed from one of the readings can create a sort of "context of ideas" for the ceremony, making both the reading and the vows more powerful.

Finding the Right Words

Even if you decide to use a line or two from a favorite song or poem within your vows, there are still all those other words to worry about. And if you're not accustomed to putting your feelings into words, you may feel stuck. You aren't; the solution you seek is no farther away than your local library or those two dusty tomes on your bookshelf that you haven't opened since high school: the dictionary and the thesaurus. Both can be a source of ideas and, perhaps more important, synonyms (words that have the same meaning). Most bookstores also offer specific reference books of synonyms.

Grab one of your references and look up the familiar words that express your feelings about your betrothed. "Love," for example. You'll find dozens of other ways to express a whole rainbow of shades and kinds of loving feelings. The precise words that articulate the nuances of your loving relationship are the ones you want to include in your vows. They will paint a picture for your future spouse and all who witness your ceremony of the unique quality of your love for one another.

Here are some of the words you might want to pick from in creating your vows:

Feelings You Have about Your Partner

love	care
passion	interest
desire	cherish
affection	hold dear
enthusiasm	prize
yearning	burn
fondness	dote upon
regard	enamored
respect	smitten
admiration	ardent
adoration	charmed
sympathy	rapturous
empathy	devoted
tenderness	lovesick
attachment	sweet for/on
fancy	head over heels in love

To You, Your Partner Is Endlessly . . .

handsome	distracting
gallant	ethical
brave	resourceful
strong	exotic
attractive	exciting
beautiful	comforting
lovely	lovable
pretty	adorable
enchanting	sweet
true	seductive
warm	winning
kind	charming
good	engaging
courageous	interesting
tender	captivating
clever	fascinating
brilliant	bewitching
witty	amiable
funny	angelic
amusing	compassionate

He/She Is Your . . .

partner	soul mate
friend	ally
lover	teammate
confidant	shoulder to lean on

Wedding Vows

flame	dear
true love	precious
paramour	pet
favorite	princess
lady love	queen
darling	king
angel	prince
goddess	knight in shining armor
betrothed	lady
beloved	man

She/He Has/Is Able To . . .

endear	seduce
charm	enamor
fascinate	enrapture
captivate	turn your head
bewitch	win your heart

You Promise To . . .

love	support
honor	encourage
cherish	obey
respect	challenge
care	lead
comfort	follow
provide	adore

trust	be loyal
listen	be true
share	be by your side
nurture	laugh

The Stuff of Vows

Once you have collected the words, phrases, lyrics, and lines that will constitute your vows, you'll need to organize them into the vows themselves. Unless dictated by your officiant or the institution in which you will wed, there are no real rules about how your vows need be structured. However, vows do traditionally have a certain logical progression to them, a structure that makes them easy for listeners to follow. Simply put, a traditional marriage vow goes something like this:

"WHO initiates with WHOM, a RELATIONSHIP specified here, which will be characterized by these PROMISES, throughout these CIRCUMSTANCES and/or until a specified POINT OF TERMINATION." (It doesn't sound very romantic put that way, but it is.)

The Traditional Format Marriage Vows Worksheet on page 146 may be a useful template for you as you begin to pull together your ideas to create your personal vows. On page 148 is the Ring Vows Worksheet.

The traditionally structured vow is merely one option; you may want your vow to be less formal, more like a monologue or speech. Even in that less defined framework, you will probably want to establish a flow to your vows, so that the focus of your expression moves organically and culminates with the thing you want to emphasize most. For a monologue or speech format vow, you may want to use a structure that

- ❊ starts with some sort of individual, personal reflection on yourself and/or your feelings about marriage before you met your intended.
- ❊ shifts focus to how your partner came into your life and the impact he or she had on you.
- ❊ is a rumination on the wonderful things about your partner, the things you love about him or her.
- ❊ is an articulation of your promises and commitment to your partner.

Marriage Vows Worksheet— *Traditional Format*

I, _____,
(your name; can be first name only, full name, or any other variation)

take you, _____,
(his or her name, can be first name only, full name, or any other variation, but should probably match form of name used above)

_____.

(for what purpose, in what manner, i.e., "as my lawfully wedded husband," "as my partner for life," etc.)

(Your promises to your partner, usually starting "I will," "I promise to," "I vow to you that I will," etc.):

_____

_____

_____

_____

_____

_____

_____ .

(The circumstances through which the pledge above will remain, i.e., "in sickness and in health," "no matter what road we travel," "wherever you are, whatever you do," "until death do us part," etc.):

_____

_____

_____

_____

_____

_____ .

Ring Vows Worksheet

(OPTIONAL: his or her name, can be first name only, full name, or any other variation)

I give you this ring,

(what the ring symbolizes or represents)

(OPTIONAL: promises to your partner): _____

_____

_____

_____

(OPTIONAL: the circumstances through which the pledge above will remain): _____

_____

_____

_____

Putting Pen to Paper

Even with a wealth of outside resources to draw upon, the average bride and groom can get a serious case of writer's block when it comes to writing their vows. Most professional writers say that even for them, the hardest part of writing is just sitting down and doing it. If, when setting out to create your vows, you are filled with the overwhelming desire to do anything else instead, know that you are not alone and that not only countless brides and grooms, but the greatest writers throughout history have endured the same struggle.

Know too that if you put your heart into them, your vows will be terrific . . . even if you think you're a terrible writer, even if you can't spell. If you've completed the worksheet, assembled your ideas and sources, but can't seem to take that next step, you might want to forget about writing for the moment and try getting your ideas together another way: by recording them. Many people who insist they can't write actually express themselves very well verbally; the words flow naturally and without worrying about subjects and verbs and adjectives, they naturally put together sentences that are interesting and grammatical. Get a tape recorder and several extra blank tapes and start talking about the one you love. You can pretend that he or she is there before you if it will help. Speak from your heart, and don't prejudge your statements. No one ever has to hear these tapes if you prefer to keep them private. You may want to do this in several "sessions" over the course of several weeks or even months. When you're ready, review the tapes, and when you find the phrases that are particularly powerful, that best express your feelings about your partner, transcribe them word for word onto paper (better yet, use individual index cards, so you can put them in the best order later). Anything that touches your emotions is likely to touch others as well, so if it moves you, makes you cry or smile, it should be transcribed. At this point you're just looking for good sentences or phrases; you don't have to worry about the order. At the end of this process you'll find that you've "written" the elements of your vows without ever having to worry about writing.

Once you have collected your cards filled with words and phrases, those you have created yourself and those you wish to include from other sources, you merely need to assemble the pieces in the best order. What is the best order? It's a highly subjective matter, but a good piece of writing, generally speaking, has a familiar, progressive build to it. Most popular songs have the same sort of structure to them: They start relatively small, with simple ideas and melodies, build gradually over the course of the song, reach a point of climax about four-fifths of the way through the song, and gradually fall back down again to a simple conclusion. If your vows are to be in a monologue or speech format, you will probably want to mimic this song structure. Even if your vows are in the more traditional format, you will probably want to order the like elements so that they are of increasing importance and significance. If you plan to promise to make your husband laugh, wipe away his tears, and love him with all of your heart for the rest of your life, you should probably put those three promises in that order, since a lot of people will probably make him laugh (not a very unique promise), a handful of close friends or family members might wipe away his tears (a moderately unique promise), but only you are pledging eternal love (a very unique promise).

As the elements fall into place, you will want to do some practice read-throughs—even if your vows aren't done yet. Watch the clock and see how you are running on time. If you and your spouse have decided to have your vows run no more than three minutes each, you may be surprised at how quickly you reach the time limit. If you're running long, you may need to make cuts. Don't know what to eliminate? Go through and rate each sentence: a definite keeper, a maybe, and not so great. Cut the "not so great" sentences and keep only the best stuff. You may have to reshuffle the order to accommodate edits. If you're running short, you'll need to find more words. Is there an idea that merits further elaboration? Add another sentence or two immediately following the introduction of that idea to give it greater weight and make your sentiments clearer.

Writing That Works

What else can you do to make your vows great? Some of the basic rules of writing will help you create vows that sparkle. They say rules are made to be broken, so don't let these guidelines keep you from writing your vows the way you want them; but if the words are just sitting on the page, you might want to consider the following:

- ❋ **Less is more.** Your fourth-grade teacher might have been impressed by your vocabulary rich in multisyllable words, but in the real world, size doesn't matter. The words you want are the ones that express what you really feel. Think of all the wonderful, meaningful one-syllable words: Love. Joy. Hope. Care. Also, presuming you're in the ballpark of your agreed-upon time length, it doesn't matter how long your vows are. A few powerful ideas succinctly expressed are all you really need.

- ❋ **Avoid generalities.** The more unique and personal the expression, the more memorable it will be—to your spouse and to those who witness your ceremony. It's fine to promise to adore your spouse forever, but it might be even more memorable to promise to adore her . . . even when she won't let you have the remote.

- ❋ **Be specific. Punctuate your vows with "real world" information.** Your wedding ceremony is not the moment to divulge your partner's most intimate quirks, but injecting a bit of your everyday lives into your vows makes them more concrete and more personal. Saying you fell in love with him when he kissed you is great, but saying you fell in love with him when the Steelers scored the tie-breaking touchdown in overtime and he picked you up and twirled you around and kissed you has more power.

* **Avoid redundancy, unless intended for a specific effect.** Try not to use the same words over and over again in each sentence. Even a powerful word like "love" can lose its significance if used repeatedly within a short statement. Consult the word lists beginning on page 142, get out your thesaurus, and find a variety of words that express your sentiments.

* **Say *the* words.** While you should avoid clichés and overused expressions, there's one familiar expression you really should consider using at some point, in some fashion: "I love you." It probably seems like a given—especially in the context of a wedding ceremony—but those three words have tremendous power, and it will mean a lot to your spouse if you go out of your way to make that simple, powerful statement at some point during your vows. (And make a point of saying it again, each and every day thereafter.)

Part 3
Practical Suggestions

Preparing for the Moment

The wedding rehearsal is so much a part of the wedding tradition that familiar rituals—from the bride's ribbon bouquet to the rehearsal dinner itself—have sprung up around it, too. But should you rehearse your vows? And how? Should you share them with your future spouse before the big day?

If you are using the standard vows of your faith, the moment of your vows may not be filled with great suspense. Don't let this be offputting—after all, the day could be filled with unexpected surprises, and you may be relieved that exchanging your vows isn't one of them. However, if you are writing your own vows, you might not want your beloved to hear them until "the" moment. Only the two of you as a couple can know which is the right way to go.

One argument for sharing the vows ahead of time is to make sure there isn't anything contained within them that might unwittingly embarrass or upset your partner. A wedding is an emotional event; the exchange of vows can be particularly dramatic. All eyes are on the couple at this big moment. The line about how you love your bride even though she steals the covers might be amusing to many, but she may blanch, worried that her dear old grandmother will be shocked that you know such a thing already.

Another concern is redundancy. While you're not creating your vows with the intention of keeping the crowd entertained, you might feel silly to share vows that are too identical.

If you have some of these concerns and wish to share your vows ahead of time, do so. If you want to speak those words to your mate only in that special moment, consider sharing the vows in writing. Here's a great way to do it:

- ❈ Each of you, individually, write your wedding vows in accordance with whatever decision you have made together about length, tone, and so on.
- ❈ On some occasion when you know you will be apart for a day or so, exchange documents. Do not read them until you are apart.
- ❈ When you are apart from one another, read the vows your partner has written. Presumably they will be wonderful, and you will be delighted and deeply moved. If not, figure out a way to kindly let your partner know your concerns. Be specific: You'd prefer it if he took out the part about how he loves it that you swear like a sailor when you break a nail. Your issues, if any, should be with content only. This is not the moment to counsel

your future mate on good grammar or point out spelling errors. Remember, it's the thought that counts. (Besides, who's going to see the spelling?)

❋ Write a letter to your partner, sharing your reaction to the vows—good and not so good. Be candid, but be kind. You'll probably find that putting your feelings on paper inspires you and moves you. And this letter is likely to be cherished by your partner for years to come.

❋ Meet with your partner to exchange letters. But don't read them or discuss the vows until you are parted again.

❋ Once away again from your future spouse, read his or her letter about the vows. If your intended has concerns about the vows you wrote, try not to take it as a personal criticism.

Regardless of whether or not you plan to share your vows ahead of time, you'll surely want to practice reading through them on your own. It really is best if you can commit them to memory. If you find memorization difficult, cut the assignment into pieces and memorize one sentence at a time, a new sentence every other day.

However, even if you have carefully memorized your vows and feel confident about your ability to deliver them when the moment arrives, you'll want to have a backup plan. Many brides and grooms decide to carry a "cheat sheet"—usually an index card—with their vows written out, which they can read from in a pinch. If you plan to carry one, be sure to create it in advance of the big moment. Use a large typeface and make sure the ink is set—particularly if you're a bride wearing gloves; you don't want to get ink smudges all over your fingers. Avoid the temptation to fiddle with your card during the ceremony. The groom might best keep his card or cards in his inside coat pocket; the bride may wish to ask the maid of honor or the officiant to carry hers.

As an alternative to the cheat sheet or cards, you may wish instead to ask your officiant to carry a copy of your vows and to prompt you verbally as needed during this portion of the ceremony, as in directed vows. This strategy helps eliminate the card shuffling, as well as the tendency many of us have to read from the cards, even though we could do just fine from memory. You'll want to gaze into your partner's eyes when you speak those special words, not look down at your scribbles. Work with your officiant to create a "system"—so he or she has your individual vows in hand at the crucial moment and knows to prompt you with a few words if you should pause significantly in your recitation or shoot him or her an anxious glance.

When you practice your vows, and when you say them on your wedding day, concentrate on speaking at a strong volume, but not shouting. Practice your best enunciation, and take care not to speak too rapidly. There's no reason to rush your vows, so take your time. You might even want to take a few deep breaths just before you begin speaking, to help you avoid the temptation to rush. Don't be afraid to let your emotions come through. You may want to note to yourself the particularly meaningful words or phrases that you want to give greatest emphasis. Without being unnatural, use dramatic pauses as well as your words to express your feelings.

Even if you don't plan to practice your vows at your rehearsal, you should take advantage of that opportunity to practice handling and speaking into the microphone, if you will be using one during your ceremony. Ask your officiant to instruct you in using the microphone, and make a mental note of the desired distance you should hold the mike from your mouth. If you are to hold the microphone yourself, handle it gently when receiving it from and returning it to the officiant, taking care not to inadvertently fill the air with those annoying microphone squeaks and squawks.

No Plan at All?

*S*ome couples opt to spontaneously pledge their vows. Although a great choice for some couples, this approach is impractical for most. Wedding day jitters can give even the most clever, conversational talker a case of the stutters. And then there's that special wedding brand of stage fright that can leave a bride or groom literally speechless. For a small informal ceremony, especially between a mature couple, spontaneous vows might be the way to go; but if you're the more typical couple, you should probably avoid improvising your vows.

If you do improvise your vows, a few words of advice:

* ❊ Keep it short. Less is more, especially when you're improvising.
* ❊ Don't talk too fast. You'll want to be understood, and speaking at a pace somewhat more slowly than you would in normal conversation will add drama.
* ❊ Don't be too funny. Really. Too often people try to go for a laugh when they are nervous. You might end up seeming glib instead of sincere. If you want

to include humor, keep it up front, toward the beginning of your vows, and make your statement from the heart.

❀ Follow the direction of your officiant. Your officiant has probably presided over numerous weddings. If you're talking too fast, or going on for too long, your officiant might prompt you to slow down or wrap it up. You shouldn't be offended—he or she has your best interests at heart.

❀ If your emotions truly get the best of you, find a way to wrap it up. If you find in the moment that pledging your love and revealing the depth of your commitment is causing you to cry buckets, you might want to wrap it up with a simple "I love you and I always will," then dry your eyes. Don't get me wrong: Strong emotion is absolutely appropriate at a wedding, but if it keeps you from being able to speak clearly, the point may be lost.

❀ Focus on your partner. After all, he or she is what it is all about. While this is a great opportunity to pledge your love in front of the witnesses gathered, your real audience is your beloved. If you are at a loss for words, just look into the eyes of the one you love and share what is in your heart.

A Lasting Reminder

Your vows are the heart and soul of your wedding day, yet if the sound system isn't good, there's a chance that the folks in the back row won't be able to hear them. For that reason, many couples share a copy of their vows, either as an addition to their program or as an element of their guest favors.

Including the vows in your program is arguably the most efficient way to share them with guests (and of course it adds to the "keepsake" quality of your wedding program); but it does, for some couples, mean one obvious drawback: The vows can be read by guests before they are spoken by the bride and groom. If you aren't worried about your guests getting a sneak preview of the vows that will be exchanged, printing them in your program is a great way to go.

If you want to share your vows with guests as an addendum to your program, you might consider having them printed on a separate sheet that can be handed out to guests as they exit the ceremony location, after the exchange of vows has been completed, and inserted into their wedding program as a part of that keepsake.

Alternatively, you may wish to include some form of your vows into your guest favors. Personalized wedding favors for guests are more popular than ever, and if you'd like to center that favor on your vows, you might consider having your vows printed on small scrolls of paper that can be affixed with ribbon to your favors.

For the bride and groom themselves, a more permanent reminder of the wedding vows is often desired. You may want to have a copy of your vows printed and mounted for display in your home. If you have written your personal vows, you might opt instead to have each of your vows, written in your own handwriting, mounted, for a truly personal keepsake.

However you choose to share or preserve your vows, a little extra work may be needed. When your vows were spoken, spelling didn't matter, but if they are to be put down in writing for everyone to see, you're going to want to make sure there aren't any misspelled words or typos. If your vows include lines from songs or literature, you will want to make sure the source is accurately noted.

Keep in mind too that your program is the ideal place to share with guests any other information that will make their experience at your ceremony more meaningful. In addition to identifying the members of your wedding party, your musical selections, and your readings, you may want to include explanatory information about any religious or cultural rituals or traditions you are including in your ceremony, especially if a large number of your guests are likely to be unfamiliar with those traditions.

Understanding the origins of symbols and rites will undoubtedly heighten your guests' enjoyment of and appreciation for your wedding ceremony.

As a final touch, you may want to include a reference to your vows in your thank-you notes. If your vows centered on a particular line from a poem or song, or a memorable turn of phrase, you may want to have stationery printed with that expression on the front of the cards upon which you will write thank-you notes to your guests after the wedding. It's a wonderful way to extend the mood and theme of your wedding celebration.

Second Weddings
and Vow Renewals

If the wedding you are planning is not your (or your intended's) first, or if your celebration is a reaffirmation or renewal of vows, your ceremony and vows may be particularly important to you. Whatever the circumstances, finding the right elements for your celebration need not be difficult; it's simply a matter of taking some time to think through the options and determining what's right for you.

"Encore" Weddings

As many as a third of all weddings each year include a bride or groom who has been married before. If the wedding you are planning is your second (or beyond), know that you aren't alone.

Although traditional etiquette once put rather strict limits on what a "proper" second wedding could be, couples today are creating the celebration they want, regardless of whether or not the bride or groom has been previously married or how many times. Still, you may

167

want to consider the traditional guidelines as you design your event. Traditionally, if the groom had been married before but it was the bride's first wedding, the celebration played out as it would for any "first wedding." If the bride had been married before, the wedding was smaller and less formal, with few, if any, attendants (because, generally speaking, the bride had already had a "big" wedding).

While those parameters need no longer be adhered to, you may want to consider other factors as you set out to create your ceremony:

* **The ages of the bride and groom.** Many encore weddings involve a couple in their forties or fifties or even beyond. While even the senior bride and groom should feel free to create the kind of event they want, most will opt for a less formal event, with a shorter guest list and few, if any, wedding attendants. Younger second-time brides and grooms will probably feel more latitude to create a "big event" wedding celebration.

* **Whether or not the bride and groom have any children, and their ages.** If the bride or groom has children from a previous relationship, a wedding is, arguably, more than just the joining of two people; a new incarnation of the family is created in the process. The full ramifications of the family situation can depend on many factors, including the ages of the children involved and to what degree they will be living with the new couple.

With the exception of the rare circumstances where a parent had no interaction with his or her child (or children), the impact on and involvement of children *must* be considered. For more on involving children in the celebration, see page 170.

❊ **The religious circumstances of your previous marriage and your desire to have your new union recognized by a religious body.** Some religious traditions have strict rules about who may or may not be married within the institution for a second time. Speak with your officiant as soon as possible to determine what, if any, procedures or paperwork might be required for you to be married within the institution (or tradition) where you wish to wed.

Of course, you will need to have completed any state-mandated divorce proceedings in order to wed. Keep in mind that your decision to marry again may have an impact on your child custody agreement (if any) and/or the financial or legal terms of your existing marital settlement. Make sure all legal and financial matters are in order well in advance of your ceremony.

A New Start

If the bride or groom has been previously married, he or she will probably want to create a wedding celebration that is notably different from a previous one. For some people, it's a matter of superstition or a desire to make a fresh start, to leave the past behind; for others it's about creating a unique event, one distinct from the wedding their family member and friends witnessed before. If the bride or groom was particularly young the first time around, he or she may feel that the plans were controlled largely by parents or in-laws; this wedding may be a chance to create a celebration that's truly personal.

Creating this new celebration will probably mean avoiding any element used in the previous ceremony that might easily be replaced this time around. Unless a particular musical selection or reading you used previously is vitally important to you, pick something different this time around. Self-written vows are particularly popular for encore weddings. You may find the perfect encore wedding vows for you among the vows starting on page 59.

You may also want to go for contrast in the size and scope of the event itself. If a previous marriage started with a formal evening wedding in a hotel ballroom, your ideal encore wedding might be an informal morning wedding in a garden. The choice is yours. Whatever the circumstances of the previous marriage or marriages, the bride and groom should work together to create the event that's right for both of them.

Involving Children

There are many reasons why you might include children in a wedding ceremony, but involving children is usually most important to the bride or groom who is bringing children from a previous marriage into a new union or the parents who are renewing their vows. While the circumstances are markedly different, and the former situation is likely to be more complicated than the latter, the ways to include children are essentially identical.

An encore wedding often involves at least one partner with children from a previous relationship. If you or your intended is bringing children into the new marriage, it is surely a matter you have discussed with regard to issues far more important than just what your wedding will be like.

Regardless of why the previous relationship ended—whether owing to divorce or the death or extended absence of the child's other biological parent—a marriage has a big impact on a child. No two children will react to the change in the same way. Generally speaking, adult children will have fewer issues with the remarriage of a parent than younger children will, but problems may arise regardless. It is essential to carefully address the larger ramifications of how a parent's remarriage will impact his or her children, and well in advance of the wedding celebration itself.

If the bride or groom has children, those children should be the first people told of the new marriage plans. If an ex-spouse is involved in that child's life, he or she should be notified as well, so that both parents can be alert to their child's emotional well-being during this potentially stressful time.

The new couple is encouraged to open their wedding

celebration to the children from a previous relationship and invite them to be as involved as they would like to be. For many children gaining a stepmother or stepfather, participation in the wedding celebration is a meaningful and rewarding experience. However, it is important to understand that participation in a parent's wedding to a new partner may be a source of considerable anxiety and guilt for a child. Discuss the matter gradually and openly with the child to determine what's right in your situation. As a remarrying parent, you may dream of having your son or daughter "stand up" for you, but you must put your child's emotional well-being above your desire to have your child play a part in your wedding celebration.

In the case of a renewal of vows or a second wedding where children are comfortable participating, the options for involving children are numerous. Among the "traditional" roles you may wish to have them perform:

* serving as acolytes or candle lighters
* escorting the bride down the aisle
* "giving away" the bride or groom
* serving as attendants
* delivering readings

Be sure to consider the range of factors that might limit a child's participation, including his or her age; ability to stand still, stay awake, or otherwise conform to the physical requirements of the ceremony; and comfort with speaking in front of a large gathering.

With the increase in encore weddings involving children, it has become common to include a short reading or exchange of words to officially recognize the new family created by the joining of the bride and groom. The parent and new stepparent may want to present a symbolic gift to the children to commemorate the event. Again, involvement in such a ritual must occur only with the explicit consent of the children involved. Don't take the effort to include children too far. It is probably not appropriate for a son or daughter to be attired as a miniature bride or groom or to receive a "wedding ring." The ceremony unites the bride and groom and, by extension, brings their respective offspring into a new family unit; it doesn't transform children or stepchildren into equal participants in the marriage itself.

In the case of the reaffirmation of vows, children will probably be delighted to join in the celebration of their parents' enduring bond. In addition to the roles just described, the children may want to make a statement of appreciation for their parents' marriage as a part of the renewal ceremony. Conversely, the parents may wish to individually recognize their children—the cherished rewards of their life together. These statements can add great sentiment to a ceremony, but exercise care that they don't go on too long or start sounding like toasts. Save the toasts for the postceremony celebration, and keep the renewal focused on the bride and groom's commitment to one another.

Reaffirming or Renewing Your Vows

Some lucky men and women exchange vows more than once—and with the same partner. Reaffirming (or renewing—there's no difference) wedding vows is an increasingly popular way for married couples to celebrate the years they have shared and to recommit themselves to one another. A renewal ceremony is sometimes planned in conjunction with a "milestone" anniversary—ten, twenty-five, and even fifty years—but it need not be an important anniversary, or an anniversary at all, for a couple to renew their vows.

In some cases, the renewal event is primarily celebratory. These couples may want to create a renewal ceremony that replicates their original wedding celebration, right down to the location, officiant, music, readings, and vows. But for many couples, the decision to renew vows has more serious implications. A couple that has weathered marital troubles may decide to renew their vows to symbolize their intent to "wipe the slate clean," start anew, and move forward, abiding more carefully by their promises. A couple that eloped, unhappily settled for a quick civil ceremony, or has grown to share a deep religious faith may want to be remarried "in the eyes of God." A couple that "married young" and spoke predetermined vows by rote may feel the need to make a more personal, mature expression of commitment and love.

The circumstances for reaffirming vows are as unique as the couples who choose to have such a ceremony, and only they can determine the right kind of event for them.

Different religious institutions have different policies about officially facilitating renewal ceremonies, so if you wish to have your celebration in a house of worship, speak with your officiant to find out the policy.

Keep in mind, too, that you may unofficially renew your vows at any time, no matter where you are. You may decide as a couple that you will privately renew your vows every year on your anniversary. Invitations need not be sent; no special attire is required. All it takes is a willing heart. Wherever you marry, whatever the circumstances, keep a copy of your wedding vows close at hand. Read them regularly, and speak them to each other once again. In good times and in bad, in sickness and in health, for richer and for poorer, your commitment to one another is what *you* make it, each and every day.

Acknowledgments

I would not have been able to write this book were it not for the support and encouragement of my family, my friends, my fellow writers and other colleagues. My thanks to my wonderful family and, most especially, my grandmothers, Catherine Schempp Smith and Lula Payne Smith. Thanks also to the good friends who supported me as I tackled this new creative challenge: Stacey Attanasio, Terry Rossio, Ken Lobb, Chris Bertolini, and Michael Hawley. My thanks to Brian Lipson and David Greenblatt for their generous and wise counsel. I owe a debt of gratitude to dozens of religious and secular officiants—too many to name here—who shared their personal insights, born of years of experience presiding over wedding ceremonies across the country, and thus made this book possible. Most of all, my thanks to my editor, Jackie Joiner, whose patience, like her brilliance, knows no bounds.

About the Author

Susan Lee Smith is a nationally recognized expert on weddings, appearing on television programs such as ABC's *Good Morning America* and NBC's *Later Today* and at bridal events in dozens of cities across the United States. She was the founding editor and producer of the WeddingChannel.com, the popular Internet wedding planning resource. A graduate of UCLA with a degree in English literature, Susan started her career in the motion picture industry, where she developed the screenplays for several hit films, and she continues to serve as a personal "writing coach" to professional and nonprofessional writers. *Wedding Vows* is her first book.